Rationality and Interpretation

Also available from Bloomsbury

Language, Identity and Symbolic Culture, David Evans
Language and Identity, David Evans

Rationality and Interpretation

On the Identities of Language

David Evans

BLOOMSBURY ACADEMIC
LONDON • NEW YORK • OXFORD • NEW DELHI • SYDNEY

BLOOMSBURY ACADEMIC
Bloomsbury Publishing Plc
50 Bedford Square, London, WC1B 3DP, UK
1385 Broadway, New York, NY 10018, USA
29 Earlsfort Terrace, Dublin 2, Ireland

BLOOMSBURY, BLOOMSBURY ACADEMIC and the Diana logo are trademarks of Bloomsbury Publishing Plc

First published in Great Britain 2022
This paperback edition published 2024

Copyright © David Evans, 2022

David Evans has asserted his right under the Copyright, Designs and Patents Act, 1988, to be identified as Author of this work.

For legal purposes the Acknowledgements on p. ix constitute an extension of this copyright page.

Cover design: Tjaša Krivec
Cover image © Victor Habbick Visions/science photo library/Getty images

All rights reserved. No part of this publication may be reproduced or transmitted in any form or by any means, electronic or mechanical, including photocopying, recording, or any information storage or retrieval system, without prior permission in writing from the publishers.

Bloomsbury Publishing Plc does not have any control over, or responsibility for, any third-party websites referred to or in this book. All internet addresses given in this book were correct at the time of going to press. The author and publisher regret any inconvenience caused if addresses have changed or sites have ceased to exist, but can accept no responsibility for any such changes.

A catalogue record for this book is available from the British Library.

A catalog record for this book is available from the Library of Congress.

ISBN: HB: 978-1-3501-9558-5
       PB: 978-1-3501-9887-6
       ePDF: 978-1-3501-9559-2
       eBook: 978-1-3501-9560-8

Typeset by Integra Software Services Pvt. Ltd.

To find out more about our authors and books visit www.bloomsbury.com and sign up for our newsletters.

Contents

Preface	vi
Acknowledgements	ix
Introduction	1
Part One The Grammar of Mind	**9**
1 Grammar and Identity	11
2 Cognition, Knowledge and Identity in Language	31
Part Two Grammar and Cultural Identity	**47**
3 Systemic Functional Grammar	49
4 Structuralism	61
Part Three Interpretation	**77**
5 Sociolinguistics and Discourse	79
6 Intersubjectivity	95
7 Narrative Identities	109
Part Four Beyond Structure	**123**
8 Phenomenology and Post Structuralism in Language	125
9 Signs and Semiotics in Identity	143
Conclusion	157
References	171
Index	177

Preface

My intention for this book is to narrate a journey of identity over linguistic paradigms and some of the multiple ways of using language. Linguistics is a broad academic area of knowledge, research and study and often seems to me very factionalized where different areas of philosophical focus have become vehemently opposed to each other. The position I adopt in the book is that these areas should complement each other, each presenting a different aspect of identity rather than become part of a zero-sum conflict in their opposition to each other. Consequently, the aim of this book is that these opposing linguistic paradigms should coexist alongside each other in terms of their different accounts of identity. So, formal linguistics would conceptualize a rational language through grammar with a concomitant rational identity located within the individual mind and would contrast with a view of language and grammar as socioculturally constituted and intersubjectively shaped. The book attempts to reconcile the two main oppositions showing them to be ultimately philosophical positions expressed through linguistics which predate linguistics in the philosophies of Descartes and Locke. To reconcile these accounts of identity and language is to concede that well yes humans have both innate mind-based qualities, which include the capacity to learn, act and create, and also intersubjective, relational qualities in both interpreting and constructing the social and cultural world.

I argue then for a more complete view of language and identity encompassing both formal, rationally based linguistics and the intersubjectivity of a more socially based linguistics where one can refer to identities rather than isolated mind-based identity. Some time ago in the linguistics corner of a social media platform, I glimpsed a comment to the effect that 'All linguistics is applied linguistics'. Yes, applied linguistics expresses the identity of the user and in lots of cases promotes social and cultural justice where languages and cultures are under threat (Uyghur culture for example in north-west China), but linguistics also theorizes on the basic intelligibility of language in how it can be understood across so many different languages. Is there a language on the planet that cannot be understood, that cannot be translated into or out of another language? I very much doubt that the known languages of the planet cannot be translated into each other even if, culturally, nuances are often lost in translation. In linguistics we have to wonder why this is the case and reflect on the hypothesis of formal linguistics that there may well be a universality in the grammatical structures of all languages. So, the book focuses upon this hypothesis as a very plausible one that needs to be examined and so, consequently I argue for a rational core within language and across all languages. A mechanical analogy would be to argue for the universal similarity of the combustion engine regardless of the make or design of the car.

In the book then language is explored both as a rational system and one generated by users, where individual use can only really be understood through reference back to the structure of the system. A word then is never isolated even if it is uttered or written as an isolated lexical item. Its full understanding is only achieved through its relations to the system of meanings which in turn draw upon sociocultural context. Similarly, the identity of the language user is never isolated but is instead understood through his/her sociolinguistic relations to the socio-linguistic system which includes the social identities of class, ethnicity, culture, gender, family, etc.

For me then formal linguistics and applied linguistics are two sides of the same coin – on one side, system, and on the other side, the user, and the book embraces both sides of the coin. The user of language draws upon both individual mental structures as well as intersubjective social structures in the interpretation and construction of meaning.

Beyond the basic binary of formal rational linguistics and linguistics of sociocultural practice, there is a range of linguistic paradigms offering different aspects of identity.

The originality of the book lies in the way in which different linguistic paradigms are brought together through the overarching theme of identity. In this way each linguistic model reflects a different facet of identity beyond the binary dichotomy of mind-based rationality and the socioculturally constituted language, both of which have been outlined above.

The book explores language as an active construal of social reality where users do more than simply reflect a pre-existing reality but actually contribute to its construction along with the construction of the identities of self within social groups. Furthermore, in cognitive linguistics the book goes beyond language itself in exploring the dialectical relation between language and extralinguistic conceptual structures.

There is also a great emphasis on intersubjectivity which questions the notion of mind as an isolated entity and proposes that individual minds are heavily populated by the voices and identities of others to the extent that there is no such thing as a sovereign, a priori mind. Some of these ideas on the identity of mind stand in opposition to each other and by bringing them together within the covers of this book we can clearly see the intellectual contradictions and the need for resolutions. The notion of narrative identity proposes such a resolution between diversification and centralization of identity/identities but we see in phenomenology and deconstruction that this proposed resolution is far from being watertight. Aspects of identities leak from the narrative and nothing is ever really, hermetically sealed, from the illusion of a totally coherent identity.

So, I believe that the attraction of the book is an original 'take' on identity which changes with each linguistic vantage point where there are no definitive right or wrong answers but rather a series of multipositional interpretations – and still a further need for researching the linguistic mysteries of identity within the substance of sameness and yet seemingly unending differentiation.

Acknowledgements

I would like to acknowledge the support and encouragement for this book by the Rev. Canon Professor Kenneth Newport Pro-Vice Chancellor (academic) and dean of the School of Education at Liverpool Hope University as well as to the University more generally.

Thanks go to the following academics who have given me informal reviews of some of the chapters in the book: Dr Patricia Giardiello, Senior Lecturer in Early Childhood Studies at Manchester Metropolitan University; Professor Steven Shakespeare, Professor of Continental Philosophy of Religion at Liverpool Hope University and Kevin Williams; Senior Research Fellow at the Institute of Education, Dublin City University. I acknowledge Father Leo Illah, Nigerian priest and native speaker of Igala for his help with research into the grammatical structures of Igala.

Thanks go to Bloomsbury linguistics editor Morwenna Scott and assistant editor Laura Gallon for their support in guiding the book through to publication and thanks also go to my daughter Sandra and my son Thomas for their enthusiastic discussion of ideas in and around the book.

This book is dedicated to the memory of my parents, Agnes and Arthur, to my wife Dominique and to my grandchildren Beatrix and Reuben.

Deo Gratias
Dr David Evans
Fellow in the School of Education
Liverpool Hope University.

Introduction

The thesis of this book draws greatly upon Bakhtin's (1981) view of language, and his view of culture more generally, in so much that it contains two forces – one centripetal, holding the centre together and the other one centrifugal, dispersing language to multiple differences and identities. The notion of identity runs parallel to language, reflecting it on the one hand as a Sameness and on the other hand as Difference. I argue in the book that identity can be defined as both sameness and difference, sameness where attributes and characteristics appear to resemble each other in word and language meanings and then, on closer inspection as in the deconstruction proposed by Derrida (1997), we begin to see the differences within sameness, making distinctions then in our word meanings. The first view of sameness is in the category of a general unitary rationality exemplified by grammatical structure and the second view is in the multiple meanings and interpretations of words and the lexical aspects of grammar or functional grammar. Towards the end of the book, in the final two chapters, I argue for a language and identity of discursive analysis to develop an analytical language about language or a metalanguage of analysis which is yet again another strand of identity shaped by language.

These two aspects of sameness and difference in language loosely correspond, respectively, to mind-based human rationality on the one hand and to the social and interpretive nature of language on the other. Therefore, language is, as I argue, both internal to mind and external to the social world simultaneously, yet at different levels, and this book's rationale is to highlight both these aspects and explore how they interrelate with identity as a corollary.

The first part of the central thesis of the book, that language is centripetal at its core, is examined in Chapter 1 in Part One titled 'The grammar of mind: Rationality'. This is predicated upon a view of language and identity as rational and mind-based, and exemplified in the work of Chomsky. It is argued in this chapter that language has a core rationality in its grammar that is common across all languages, and examples of grammatical constructions are taken from

Basque and Igala grammar to explore this. I have chosen to use Basque as a short basic empirical case study in grammatical rationality because it is a non-Indo-European language and therefore unrelated to other European languages that surround it which are all Indo-European in origin. Further to this, it does not share evolutionary origins with any other known language. I have also chosen Igala, an African language from Nigeria to explore claims for the universal nature of basic grammar. Again, this is a very short case study with examples of sentences that have an intelligible structure for an English native speaker. Both languages, in their basic grammar, have a basic cognition from the standpoint of English even though Basque is a free-flow case-marking system in its grammar whereas Igala is a fixed subject verb object word order tonal language yet not unlike English and French in its written grammar.

Grammatical rationality is the basis for Chomskyan Universal Grammar, however not a new concept, but one which draws upon a Cartesian view of mind and also the Port Royal grammarians' view of language, in the sixteenth century, as structurally innate and mind-based.

Chapter 2 continues the theme of rationality in language although not in the core grammar but in linguistic statements and their correspondence with the outside world in the concept of truth statements. Here I draw upon the work of Wittgenstein in the Tractatus and then, subsequently his revised opinions of language as language games in his later work Philosophical Investigations. I continue the chapter with a section on cognitive linguistics drawing upon mind-based conceptualizations that feed into language. Cognitive linguistics moves away from the idea that meaning is contained just in language itself, stating that conceptual structures, located outside of the language area of mind, are partly responsible for the development of meaning.

The second part of the thesis that language is simultaneously a centrifugal force, therefore a divergent force, propelling away from the centre, is explored from Chapter 3 in Part Two onwards. Reference as to where we are situated in the progression of the book will be made in an introductory section at the beginning of each chapter. However, in a brief general overview, the Systemic Functional Grammar of Chapter 3 in Part 2 titled 'Grammar and cultural identity' moves away from a Chomskyan view of inner rational grammar to suggest that grammar does indeed respond to social context in its composition in such as gender, number and the concealment of agency. There is also a view in the linguistic perspective of Structural Functional Linguistics that we choose language to construct the world as well as, at the same time, language being a representation of the world. Chapter 4 focuses on Saussurean Structuralism in terms of words and their meanings. We see the interplay between words as signifiers and culture objects as signified and how meanings and identities are not an essential a priori but rather change in their connection with each other over time.

Part Three titled 'Interpretation', comprising Chapters 6, 7 and 8, focuses on interpretation and the identity of the language user as opposed to language itself. Chapter 5 explores identities in terms of ideologies in language and the way in which individuals construct themselves and others through language. It also introduces notions of power as a factor in the construction of identity and ideology through discourse. Chapter 6 explores how discourse and utterances contain the voices of others through the notion of heteroglossia, thereby suggesting that language does not express a single unitary identity but rather multiple identities through different voices, often powerful ones. Discourse colonization is examined in terms of the notion of power behind and within discourse. Chapter 7 brings different voices together in Ricoeur's notion of narrative identity. Ricoeur's rationale for this is that, despite the disparate subjective positions that individuals traverse in their lives, they seek coherence in a narrative identity which amounts to the construction of a life story. This is an assertion of individual free will in a desire to create coherence in a narrative out of what might be the incoherence of experience. The argument against this is that the metanarrative necessary for this coherence can be construed as just another discourse or text amongst others and still leaves the individual 'ungrounded'. Ricoeur's response to this is that narrative identity can only be authentic where ethical linguistic behaviours lead to ethical action and so where both are closely connected together in a linguistic performative causality. Ricoeur states that the coherence of narrative is penetrated by future possibilities of identity as becoming characterized by the difference in alterity. The future is an otherness, the alterity of other subjects in intersubjectivity represents otherness which Ricoeur names 'ipse' of being as becoming as opposed to 'idem' as the substance of stable being. Narratives therefore have to be open to the world because they necessarily embody otherness. This is because when we speak, we index the future in day-to-day life referring to possible ways of being over time and we bring this forward into the present. Our present tense speech often in this way evokes the future. For example, if one asks someone, 'Where are you going?' or 'What are you doing?' eliciting 'I am ….ing', this present continuous reply is in itself journeying into the future, albeit the immediate future.

The construction of identity is recognizing this 'deconstruction' between 'idem' and 'ipse' and trying to resolve it as we attempt to construct coherence in narrative identity which is always subject to some change and destabilization.

Part Four – 'Beyond structure' – focuses on post structuralism starting with the phenomenology of Bergson leading to the deconstruction project of Derrida in Chapter 8. The aim of this chapter is to show that in contrast with the preceding section and chapter, identity is constituted by difference and deferral. This means that if we look closely enough outside of the more powerful constraints of sameness, we see that areas of sameness can be subdivided into differences, so that beyond the ready-to-hand easily visible sameness there is difference. An analogy of this would be soldiers in uniform where prevailing power constrains individuals into a sameness, yet beneath the uniform, military standard haircuts and drill, we can see on closer inspection the differences of the men and women as individuals. This does not mean to say that sameness is not a real identity because it serves no doubt a functional purpose; it just means that the sameness of the coherent narration does not paint the fullest picture. So, for the fuller picture, one has to deconstruct and unpick the top layer of sameness to see the individual and marginalized differences underneath. Language is a constitutive element of this where the military language in uniform objectifies, not only the body of the soldier but also his/her linguistic references in the use of clear instrumentalized language. Of course, out of uniform the soldier will probably speak nothing like this, and his/her language is likely to reflect his/her individual personality differences.

Again, even the differences can subdivide into further differences and reflected in language, this might mean dialects, regional accents and the lexicon of special interests.

Identity here is not just based on the sameness/difference dichotomy but also on deferral in the idea that, due to the passage of time and the fact that we are inside of time as duration, an idea proposed by Bergson, our identity not only subdivides into identities but continually changes as it moves forward. So, we may be not exactly the same person as we were thirty years ago. A key philosopher in this chapter apart from Henri Bergson is Jacques Derrida who is the author of deconstruction. In Chapter 8 we learn that deconstruction is a process of which the ingredients reside in the sameness of identity and arise from a combination of deferral and difference. Derrida combines these two terms into his own neologism of 'Différance' spelt with an 'a' instead of an 'e'. We see that Derrida takes up the notion of time from Bergson because we live in time as a duration, and we develop and evolve our identity within it. Things change with time – identities change, meanings of statements and words change as the reader interprets texts differently. The sameness of an identity or a meaning contains its own difference, and in deconstruction, deferral and difference as différance (with an 'a'!) come to the surface. According to Royle (2000; p11), deconstruction is 'what makes every identity at once itself and different from itself'. So, everything is divisible when released from the constraining power at the centre where hegemonic and unitary static identity are illusory, but often held together by social power and perhaps useful for instrumental purposes at moments in time. I refer here to the individual who draws upon a conventionally accepted identity as in a CV for a job application. This presents a coherent professional and social identity but does not tell us everything there is to know about the individual's identity.

Therefore, we see, in this chapter, that identity can be sameness but there will be also, within sameness, emerging differences.

Chapter 9 explores the world of signs as the semiotic nature of language and identity. The philosophy of the American philosopher Charles Sanders Peirce is outlined here whose seminal ideas underpinned semiotics in the same way that Saussure provided the foundation for linguistics. Signs are introduced as a part of language and indeed many linguists refer to language and sign since many people speak using physical gesture to enhance communication and often facial and other bodily gestures contain meaning on their own account, more especially in sign languages such as Makaton. In some ways this chapter expresses the book's dichotomy between the unity of language and identity and the difference and dispersal of identity. This is seen in the difference between, on the one hand, signs that have an inner identity, such as natural signs, in terms of making something other than themselves known and, on the other, signs that are their own meanings that proliferate in a world of leisure and lifestyle to produce their own ideal worlds of fantasy and, eventually the moving interactive images of virtual reality. Both language and signs in their different definitions and paradigms throughout the book have implications for the construction of identities as ways of being in the world.

The chapter argues for a way back from being lost in a virtual fantasy world and fragmented identities by proposing, within education and development, a critical discursive language of analysis. By espousing a critical discourse analysis within education, individuals can regain the ascendency of free will over an uncritical deterministic acceptance of media images and slogans.

Finally, the Conclusion includes some implications for education in terms of not only expansive multiple identities of language and culture but also multilayered identities including a discursive language of analysis. In this way rationality and interpretation within language and identity are brought into relationship with each other.

A key element in the book is to settle on a definition of identity. As already mentioned, I propose from the outset a working definition of identity generally as bearing the notion of belonging through sameness in the context of difference. There is then difference within sameness and deconstruction is the Derridean project which brings this difference to the surface.

Royle (2000), to restate, defines Derridean deconstruction as 'what makes every identity at once itself and different from itself' (2000; p11). This definition is inspired by the concept of deconstruction (Chapter 8), however this is built upon Saussurean structuralism (at the midpoint of the book in Chapter 4), where we see language categories in the naming of objects, showing that an understanding of a named category lies both in sameness and difference. Firstly, a category can only be named as a category because of its external difference from other categories and secondly because this category contains within it, elements that resemble each other, or internal sameness. We will understand that even within sameness, on further examination, further differences may occur which then develop into their own subcategories. There is no reason why such sub-categorical sameness should not continue subdividing into smaller and smaller categories. Royle (2003) argues that Derrida, the author of deconstruction, does not deny structuralism since one needs the centre within structures in order to deconstruct. Derrida's work indeed was built upon the foundations set out by Ferdinand de Saussure, the father of structural linguistics.

Identity therefore arises out of an interplay between sameness and difference; however, deconstruction, as we shall see in Chapter 9 and the Conclusion, transcends structuralism in stating that every unity is divisible and so identity is always incomplete and therefore on-going.

As the book moves from the identities of sameness and difference in language towards language use, the same modality for the definition of identity will apply to language users. Here we see users of language define themselves in line with the varieties of language they use in their different discourses expressing their difference, whilst at the same time seeing the commonality in humanity expressed in language containing inner rational coherence.

This introduction is written based on a rationale that the book will be a journey in language and identity and that identity is not likely to be unitary and forever the same. So, at this point at the start of the book, having researched much of the literature for a book plan, I think the general notion of identity as a categorical belonging, born in sameness and difference is a useful starting point.

Of course, the understanding of identity issues will develop as the book unfolds, so for example this happens when categories of sameness are seen in themselves to contain difference. This is likely to destabilize identity as unitary and simply transform the singular entity into the plural or multiple identities. Then we will have to consider the identities of those who speak many languages and engage in multiple discourses, and this will become more apparent as language and its use are refined in the coming chapters. From a starting point where identity is defined and justified at the outset as a category of sameness and difference, it will be interesting to see where we end up on our arrival at the concluding chapter. But first let's embark on the journey.

Part One

The Grammar of Mind

1

Grammar and Identity

This section explores the role of grammar in the formation of a rational identity as opposed to a social or cultural identity. It will be seen that this basic identity is rational and mind-based and, in this chapter, expressed directly into language, based upon universal grammar. According to Chomsky, universal grammar occurs across languages although ultimately, if this is to be accepted as a scientific feature of language as opposed to a conjecture or assertion, the proposition of universal grammar needs to be explored empirically rather than existing as a philosophical inference of necessity. Universal grammar as a philosophical proposition nonetheless attempts to answer the question of what accounts for language being intelligible between users of the same linguistic code and, also across different languages in translation. The chapter attempts to explore basic grammar between two completely unrelated European languages, English in the Indo-European lineage and Basque which has no relations with Indo-European languages. I also explore grammatical features between English and Igala, an African language spoken in Nigeria. The rationale for this is to demonstrate that there is intelligibility at a basic level between small-scale data sets taken from two languages, unrelated to English. This is of course exploratory since the aim of this book is not to attempt any proof of universal grammar but simply to show a basic common identity in exploring some fundamental grammatical relations between unrelated languages.

Consequently, relations between Universal Grammar and the diversity of operational surface grammar are explored through the notion of principles and parameters which we see in the chapter accounting for flexibility in syntax or applied grammar.

Introduction

There exists within linguistics in its broadest sense a tension between the notion of a central necessity for language to be internally intelligible and its external cultural diversity. So, this tension plays out between a concept of inner rationality of the linguistic core, close to the notion of mind itself and the exterior reaches of variety, difference and consequently interpretation.

This dichotomy has not just emerged randomly within the broad sphere of linguistics but rather reflects a philosophical dichotomy that has existed since the Enlightenment, constructed around the relationship between the individual's relationship to social context and his/her internal learning capacity. Locke and Descartes were the proponents of this dichotomy in viewing the individual respectively as a 'blank slate' where learning comes from context to the individual or conversely starts from the individual's mind itself. These are basically two versions of the individual, either mind-based or a social agent. We can see this played out in the subject of linguistics in terms of theoretical and applied sociolinguistics.

In this book, we explore the relationship between the two and examine the extent to which they are interrelated rather than existing in a 'zero-sum' stand-off. This means exploring language as both structure and culture, rather than as mutually exclusive and asking whether, or not the borders between the two are porous, and therefore influencing each other. Does culture for example influence structure or is culture constructed upon a basic structure, in the same way that, by analogy, the cultural-aesthetic design of a vehicle is constructed around the engine and transmission? In other words, does language operate from the inside outwards or from the outside inwards? Underpinning this dichotomy is still the basic Cartesian-Lockean divide and whether, or not, there is a bridge or compromise between the two. To answer this question, we need, firstly, to analyse what makes sentences or utterances intelligible and how we are able to move between languages, as opposed to being imprisoned within one language. This is because even though different languages present different surface grammatical aspects in such as verb tenses (or no verb tenses at all but rather time prepositions) and word orders, they can be translated between each other, even though not always perfectly mapped on to each other. The fact that languages can be translated may suggest common basic structures but because they cannot be mapped onto each other exactly may also suggest cultural differences in content beyond the basic structures. This idea might suggest both structure and semantics operating closely within language. So secondly, later in the book, we will need to explore the interrelations between the inside and the outside of language and the extent to which external semantics might act upon linguistic structures. Chapter 3 on systemic functional grammar in Part Two titled 'Grammar and cultural identity' will explore the interrelationship between grammar and semantics.

Structural rationality

Language can be considered knowledge and Chomsky (2009) refers to ideal linguistic knowledge as competency. This is the knowledge acquired by an individual regardless of performance and is the language, through its acquisition, that the individual comes to know.

This view of language as knowledge has roots going back at least as far as Descartes who viewed knowledge of the world as being contained in the structures of mind (Moriarty 2008). Unlike Locke, Descartes did not view the mind as a 'blank slate' (Locke 2010–15) but rather containing structures which reflected the structures of knowledge in the outside world and in this way the individual is able to connect with and make sense of the outside world. Therefore, the individual does not have to learn the world from a cold start but simply acquires that which lies within the structures of mind in relation to the world.

On the other hand, Locke simply maintains that all that we **do** have as innate is simply a general capacity for learning and retention but this is generic to all learning and not mapped onto the world in an innate structural relationship.

In the 1600s the Port Royal grammarians took up the Cartesian epistemology and applied it to language. In modern times Chomsky has resurrected this view of language and acquisition and revolutionized linguistics, rescuing it from the stimulus–response of behaviourism. This was indeed a step forward but is nonetheless fraught with a lack of empirical evidence. Indeed, Chomsky bases much of his linguistic philosophy upon English, leaving the field open for others to make connections with other languages.

Chomsky (2009) takes a philosophical position by asking what are the necessary conditions to make sentences intelligible? Sentences are strings of words and therefore there must be an underlying structure to create a meaningful coherence from them. We are consequently intelligible to each other although we might say that this is due to a shared culture and that linguistic structures are a function of shared culture rather than isolated mind. Grammar might then be organizational patterns of words which orientate meaning and which, in a shared culture, have built up over time. A different language might have evolved different word patterns to shape grammar over time. If we compare languages there is truth in this, as we can see in the following example between French and English:

'Je lui donne le stylo. I give her the pen'. We notice a slight difference in grammatical word order which word for word reads, 'I to her give the pen'. This becomes a little more complicated in word order if we combine the indirect object pronoun of lui- 'to her' with the direct object pronoun of 'it' -le, in order to state, 'I give her it or I give it to her'. This translates in French as 'Je le lui donne' or 'I it to her give'. However, we can argue that this is only cultural grammar at surface level and is the culture that resides within language. Nevertheless, even if all the word orders change, we can still work out what they mean because of our conceptual grammar or as Chomsky calls it 'Universal Grammar' (Chomsky 2009). It is therefore necessary to focus our attention on the deeper structures of grammar, not where grammar interacts with cultural vocabulary but where grammar interacts with mind in such a manner that we can call it conceptual grammar. 'Philosophical grammarians maintain that languages vary little in their deep structures, although with wide variations in surface manifestations' (Chomsky 1968). This suggests that indeed grammar is universal within mind at a deep level, at the psychological level of human cognition although it translates into cultural patterns at surface operational level. Chomsky declares that Universal Grammar contains 'whatever aspects of language are intrinsic to the human mind –'(Cook & Newson 2007; p49)

Since, in this model, conceptual grammar is a part of human psychology, we acquire language rather than actively learn it. Chomsky and his associate Lenneberg (1967) cite as evidence the ease with which children at a young age can 'learn', not only their own native language but also any language, as long as they are exposed to it, much in the same way as plants will grow given the right conditions. This is probably the closest analogy, that of organic growth in optimal conditions. A tree or a plant is not taught to grow; it just does so of its own innate momentum so long as there are sufficient water, light and soil nutrients. To continue within this analogy, the plant has grown from a seed and the 'blueprint' for all the plant's growth is contained entirely within the seed and the minimal eternal conditions required for its growth do not cause the growth but enable and optimize it.

Chomsky's concept to underpin this is named 'Poverty of Stimulus' where with the minimal of favourable environmental conditions, children will master any language, to which they have been exposed, by a very young age. Consequently, we do not really learn language but grow into it as grammar grows in the mind. By contrast Halliday's position (2002) is that there is not 'a priori' language learning module or structure awaiting autonomous development but rather a human propensity to learn from sociocultural and linguistic context. Here language and learning lie within the social environment and its interaction with the sociocultural individual rather than uniquely within mind.

Chomsky's universal grammar and Halliday's systemic functional language

Bavali and Sidighi (2008) argue that Chomsky's Universal Grammar and Halliday's Systemic Functional Grammar can complement each other rather than stand in opposition. Unlike Universal Grammar or henceforth UG, Halliday's notion of grammar exists at surface level and arises out of sociocultural use arising from everyday social practice. Grammar is lexicogrammar, constituted by our use of language and not from the isolated unitary mind. If we consider Chomskyan and Hallydayan models of language, and language acquisition as innate on the one hand and, on the other hand, as social learning, then this dichotomy is not far removed from the Descartes–Locke dichotomy between mind and society that was mentioned earlier.

Chomsky insists that there is a separation between semantics and structure whereas for Halliday it is the opposite in that meaning shapes grammar. It is true that at the level where Halliday situates grammar, social meaning shapes grammatical structure. Consider the following example: 'All staff are expected to attend all meetings at all times, on time'. Now this might be considered by employees to be a very harsh decree, constraining the freedom of the individual in a society where freedom is important and, undoubtedly, one person or a group would be responsible for promulgating such a statement. The passive voice, however, exculpates agency by hiding it in the grammar. Agency has disappeared and, with it, moral responsibility, and so the sentence, in the passive voice, is turned into an injunction disconnected from personal agency. Grammatical structure in this case has been shaped by the ideological or political environment. For Chomsky, however, there is a deeper grammar which is totally structural, and which can help the situation, and this could be as follows: object verb subject; since there is an object ('all staff') and action ('are expected to attend'), there has to be a subject, in a subject–object causation. We can see the object in 'All staff' and we know this, because the staff are not the agents who are 'expecting'. We can see the action in 'expected to attend' and so there must conceptually be a subject even though it is a hidden category. Employees can then ask who the subject is, issuing this decree and who is therefore responsible, rather than implicitly accepting a command disguised as fact that hides power. It seems that such an example may well highlight the interrelation between mind-based rational grammar and social grammar. The rational, conceptual grammar contains empty categories which can be filled with a metalanguage such as agency, causality/intentionality, action, direct or indirect object of action. Therefore, by referring surface language back or upwards to these extralinguistic categories we can conceptualize more readily what is being written or stated rather than becoming trapped within language itself. We can see then in this simple example, how, in the notion of an absent category, Universal Grammar can underpin surface grammar, thereby making explicit that which is hidden.

At a simple childlike level, an infant or toddler might say to her/his father, 'What doing daddy?' The underlying grammar assumes 'are you' at the surface due to this being a hidden empty grammatical category. We can understand this because we possess these empty categories in our Universal Grammar. We know therefore when agency is missing because this is part of our thinking if not actual language. Chomsky asserts as follows: 'Linguistic theory, the theory of UG – is an innate property of the human mind' (1976; p34).

According to Bavali and Sidighi (2008), Halliday himself accepts that language cannot be fully understood from within, but in Halliday's case, the extralinguistic referral to understand text is a recourse to the metalanguage of discourse, genres and registers within social structures rather than the metacognition of mind.

Chomsky himself, in fact, does not list an inventory of the universals contained in his Universal Grammar and declares UG is a 'component of the theory of mind but as an abstraction' (1976; p43). Consequently, one of the main criticisms made of him is that his linguistic philosophy does not emerge from any empirical research. His position is a philosophical one of the necessary conditions for sentences to make sense in languages and for children to be able to learn those languages so easily, often from minimal optimal conditions or poverty of stimulus. Therefore, if one asks the question, 'Why is language the way it is and what are the necessary conditions for language?', the logical response is to justify language from outside language, to find the underpinning justification. Otherwise, to refuse to do so is the same as expressing a tautology in saying 'language is like this because it is'. Language, in this way, cannot explain itself, but whereas Halliday would refer to social language and discourse for explanation, Chomsky refers to mind.

I would then argue that UG could be considered an active process of conceptualization and metacognition of surface language and grammar in action rather than a fixed entity of mind. Certain universals may emerge from this, such as agency, action, time, intention, object but these should be seen as emerging out of an active process of extralinguistic conceptualization, an ongoing metalanguage of enquiry rather than as static a priori universals.

If UG as a grammatical conceptualization is a process, then we can see this in action when translating between radically different languages where surface word orders and grammars are very different. I have quoted the case of translating between French and English with slightly different word orders, but these are languages which, coming from the same Indo-European root, are related to each other.

In the next section I consider Basque, which is a non-Indo-European language, uniquely unrelated to any other language, in order to explore how we are able to refer surface level grammatical difference to metalinguistic conceptualization in order to gain understanding in English. I propose this metalinguistic exploration as an empirical method of locating a commonality of grammatical identity between unrelated languages.

The case of Basque: Locating identity within and between languages

If language is the 'House of Being' as Heidegger claims (Basic Writings 1993), then at surface level, speakers of Basque and English would be locked inside their respective languages, living totally different social realities – a prospect also proposed by the linguistic determinism of Sapir and Wharf (Hussein 2012). This may be partially true since there are meanings which between languages are 'lost in translation', so we use the foreign word because there is no English equivalent. Here I refer to concept words such as 'Schadenfreude', 'Détente', 'Esprit de Corps' 'Hwyl' 'Gusto' 'Machismo' to quote from German, French, Welsh and Spanish/Italian respectively. Occasionally these foreign words are appropriated by the native language to develop a slightly different meaning (Gusto used in Spanish/Italian and English have slightly different meanings; in Spanish it is pleasure or liking; taste in Italian whereas in English it has become a vigorous enthusiasm). So, there is a sense in which certain different social realities are shaped by the different languages which construct them. This is the cultural content of language which will be explored in later chapters.

At issue here however in translating between languages is the location of 'self' and identity. If as Heidegger (1993) maintains that 'Language is the House of Being', then we can have different identities in different languages. However, we need to consider the location of 'self' as we move between languages, especially when the languages are very different and occasion some difficulty in translation. I would suggest that this evokes an analytical metaidentity where we conceptualize across different structures. In this sense we can have a structural self or identity and a cultural one at different levels.

If we were to translate Basque into English, word for word, it would make little sense as we see in the following examples:

'Nire aitarekin' translates word for word as 'my father with'. A minor rethink gives us 'with my father'.

A more difficult task would be to translate the following from Basque: 'Katuak txoria jaten du' which is rendered word for word as 'Cat the bird the eating it is'. We know the English words, but we have to work out who or what is doing what to who/what. Otherwise, the word-for-word translation makes no sense. We can use common sense to work out that the cat is more likely to eat the bird than vice versa and so we have 'the cat eats the bird', however, if we substituted the Basque word for 'fox' instead of 'bird' we might not be able to fall back on common sense and we would have to conceptualize the grammar. So, we will do this with the Basque word for 'fox' in the following sentence 'Azeriak katua jaten du'. Translating word for word we have 'Fox-the, cat-the-eating it is' but we need to know what is eating what?

In Basque nouns have endings for the definite and indefinite articles as well as case endings for the subject of a transitive verb. The subject of a transitive verb ends in -k, so we know that Azeriak-the fox is subject of the sentence. The object does not have an ending, so we know that katua is the object; '-a' is 'the' so 'katua' is the cat and also object of the verb and so we know the 'the fox eats the cat'.

In working out this sort of translation, we might say that understanding is moving between the two languages in a metaidentity at a conceptual level. The conceptualization is outside of either language to solve the problem as if it were not; we would not be able to move away from the nonsense word-for-word translation.

Of course, Basque-English bilinguals know both languages so well, they can operate at the level of the socially outward-facing language. Beginners, however, need to use extralinguistic cognitive processes. This involves a conceptualization of who or what is the subject of the sentence, who or what is the object and which of the words is the verb and in which tense. These features of subject, verb, object or in other words, agency, causation, action, object of action, might be considered universals in a process which becomes evident in the problem solving of moving between languages which one might not know very well. The more uncertain we are about the languages in question, the more metalanguage and metacognition are called into action.

We can see this again in the following example again drawn from Basque:

Gizona kalean erori da
Man-the, street-the, in, fallen-he/she has

Note that 'the man' here 'gizona' does not have a 'k' ending and so is NOT 'gizonak' because 'the man' is not the subject of a transitory verb since 'has fallen' does not take a direct object.

Again, at first word-for-word view, a translation would be confusing and if this were a much more complex and longer sentence, a translation would be impossible without being able to decipher some universals such as subject, verb and object, direct or indirect. We need to undertake an analysis if we do not know the language in order to work out what is happening and, in doing this, one's identity is analytical moving above each language. Again, Basque grammatical rules indicate that the definite article goes after the noun with the suffix – 'a' being 'the'. So 'gizona' is 'the man'. There is a prepositional case of 'in' being 'n' as a suffix. The street is kalea (with the 'a' ending for 'the') and 'in the street' 'kalean'. Finally, the verb always comes at the end. So 'erori da' is 'fallen he/she has'. The final translation is then 'the man has fallen in the street'.

The next example is slightly more complicated involving more grammatical concepts than the previous sentence. Let us consider the following example:

Emakumeak gizonari katua eman da.

Where the word for word translation is-

Woman-the, man-the-to, cat-the, given he/she has.

Again we know because of the 'a' suffix that it is 'the' woman and furthermore we can know that 'the woman' is the subject of a transitive verb because of the 'k' suffix, so that we have 'emakumeak'. We know that 'the cat' is a direct object of the verb because it does not have any case ending – it is simply 'katua' 'the cat'. The verb as usual is at the end of the sentence so 'has given' is 'eman da'. Finally, 'to the man' is 'gizonari'; 'the man' being 'gizona' and the dative case 'to' being 'ri'.

So, we have 'The woman has given the cat to the man' and not 'The man has given the cat to the woman'.

Trask (1997) points out that in Basque 'The order of major phrases is quite free, and variation is used for thematic purposes' (1997; p122). He also says that

'Basic word order is SOV' (subject, object, verb. – my parenthesis), but this order is far from rigid, and all other word orders may occur, though the verb headed ones are uncommon. Trask gives four-word orders for the English sentence, 'John hit Peter' which are as follows:

1 Jonek Kepa jo zuen – where 'Jonek' is John, 'Kepa' is Peter and 'jo zuen' is hit.
2 Kepa Jonek jo zuen
3 Kepa jo zuen Jonek
4 Jo zuen Jonek Kepa (Trask 1997; p109)

We can see then that word order does not matter because the case ending of 'k' in 'Jonek' tells you that this has to be the subject of the sentence and the lack of case ending in 'Kepa' means it has to be the object of the verb. Therefore, word orders in sentences do not have an underlying grammatical function, as in English and French for example, because the case endings denote the grammatical functions of the words. Every word has its grammatical place which the translator into English can locate, since across languages there is an underlying concept of agency or subject; direct or indirect object; action and causation, i.e., that there is a cause–effect between agent, action and the object. These concepts exist between English and Basque alongside other concepts that can be understood across these languages such as dative, genitive, time, adjectives, etc. even though English and Basque are two completely unrelated languages with different word orders.

Let us keep John or Jon as the subject and now say that, when in a better mood, 'John has visited the museum in San Sebastian yesterday'. We must keep in mind that word position in Basque is flexible because of its case endings and so, unlike English or French, word order does not necessarily play a part in Basque grammatical meaning.

The first way of expressing this is as follows: Atzo Jonek museoa bisitatu du Donostian where a word-for-word translation into English would be Yesterday Jon museum visited he has San Sebastian-in. (N.B. Donostia is Basque for San Sebastian; the 'n' is the suffix for 'in', so in San Sebastian is Donostian).

The same sentence can have the following five different word orders in Basque

1 Atzo Donostian Jonek museoa bisitatu du
2 Atzo Donostian museoa bisitatu du Jonek
3 Jonek atzo museoa bisitatu du Donostian
4 Jonek museoa bisitatu du Donostian atzo
5 Jonek bisitatu du museoa atzo Donostian.

I would agree with Chomsky (2011) that language is a conceptual system alongside a communicative system. The sentences above are conceptually coherent even though at surface level, they do not appear to make sense. We can work out what they mean because the case endings and verb endings can be conceptualized by our internal processes. If the surface language were the only resource we had, without recourse to a metacognition, the sentences would have no meaning for us because our English or French or Spanish grammars reside partially in word orders. We could run the sentences as empty grammatical categories substituting the semantics of the vocabulary with structures such as 'x', 'y' and 'z' where 'x' is the agent, 'y' is the action and 'z' the direct object as a linear grammatical structure. However, with case endings as in Basque, x, y and z could run in any order as long as each element was marked with its grammatical subject-object conceptual designation, no matter where they were located in the sentence. In other words, the empty grammatical categories would provide a structural meaning in themselves without the lexical semantics. We see then that sentences, as well as being items of communication, are also at the same time conceptual tools, helping us to understand the world and thereby language serves a dual function, communication and conceptualization.

Case study of basic sentence syntax of Igala

Igala is an African language spoken in Nigeria by 2 million people. It is a tonal language with regard to word meaning in that, words with the same spelling can have different meanings according to voice tone with three tones of low, middle and high. Verb tenses are also expressed by tone. Nevertheless, sentence syntax (syntax being the arrangement of words in a grammar to form a sentence or utterance) is as important as in any other language.

The rationale of this section, as in the last section, is to see the basic grammar commonalities between an Indo-European language such as English and in this case study, Igala. We will see that although there are surface differences in some word orders in that adjectives follow nouns and definite articles also follow nouns, the principal word order is subject verb object or S.V.O. English and French, the languages that this book has used throughout are also S.V.O.

We must bear in mind again that Chomsky maintains that the underlying grammar or Universal Grammar of all languages is the same with the only variations existing at the surface, in line, in my view, with the cultural practices of the country in which the language is spoken. Chomsky himself, of course, says nothing about language and culture.

Kemmener (2015) states that both Subject, Verb, Object and Subject, Object, Verb languages start with the subject as head because subject agency tends, in most cases, to precede object as this position reflects, the 'temporal flow of energy from agent to patient' (2015; p150). Logically then languages that write from right to left would have a subject head but going in a different direction. This would be a matter of research for syntax in those languages.

However, our previous study has demonstrated that Basque is subject lead in a Subject, Object, Verb basic word order but with many variations. Basque is a free-flowing word order and word orders are not so essential because of its case ending. The subject of the sentence always has a 'k' ending so indeed it could occur anywhere in the sentence in theory. Nevertheless, Kemmener argues in favour of a 'subject salience' to highlight active agency on a passive object recipient where the verb phrase of verb and object remain contiguous but passive. So, word order syntax in all languages is an essential part of grammar and Akamajian (1995) contends that no matter how free a language is in word order, there will always be word order constraints. If we take Basque into account, there may well be some debate about this latter point. Halliday (1985) however argues that all languages have a logical order for the combination of linguistic structures in which the different elements play different roles.

In the following case study, in examples of basic word order in Igala, the objective is to look for logical meaning from an English language standpoint in a word-for-word translation. Is there a logic that can then be rendered into a fluent native speaker English? The exercise takes place in two moves, firstly the Igala sentence in word-for-word translation and secondly the completed translation into a fluent native speaker English.

Here are ten examples of basic sentences in Igala:

1 Fred a gba otakada
  Fred is reading a book
  Note: a gba – is reading; olakada – a book; no indefinite article. One move translation.

2 Jenny a gba otakada le
  Jenny is reading book the
  Jennny is reading the book
  Note: the definite article follows the noun.

3 John wa emi onale
   John came here yesterday
   Note: straight word-for-word translation in past tense

4 Jenny che ukolo onale
   Jenny do work yesterday
   Jenny worked yesterday

5 John ko unyi efufu le
   John builds house white the
   John builds the white house
   Note: the definite article follows the noun and adjective and the adjective of colour also follows the noun. Present tense sentence

6 Omi a che ukolo
   I am is do work
      I am working

7 Omi a che ukolo onale
   I am is do work yesterday
      I worked yesterday

8 Abimoto le a che iya
   Children the is do play
   The children are playing

9 Omi che iya
   I am do play
      I am playing

10 Omi a che iya onale
   I am do play yesterday
      I played yesterday
   Note: past tense is denoted through time expression 'yesterday'.

Apart from the linguistic basic rational identity in the language composition, there is also a rational process of identity in the translating from one language to another. This is a reasoning process requiring a metaidentity and meta language external to both languages in order to explore understanding of what is being expressed within the different word orders. The translator is indeed looking for the underlying grammar logic before resurfacing with a native speaker understanding and fluent rendering in the host language.

Language as conceptual understanding

Vygotsky (1986) also, from a different tradition, points out that children use language as a conceptual tool, in trying to consolidate understanding, through the use of inner speech when undertaking tasks or when at play. This is not language as a communicative tool but rather as a conceptual tool. Adults may also do this in order to retain an understanding of one element of a problem as a basis for progression to another level. My argument then is that language has universal conceptual features which consolidate and progress understanding. Vygotsky (1986) argued indeed that language and conceptual thought have two different origins that start to come together at around two years of age. There are examples of individuals using words even beyond childhood without knowing their full meaning, because they have repeated what they have heard at conversational level without cognizance of meaning. Therefore, the connection between the word phoneme and a meaning requires a conceptual system, which, according to Vygotsky, can then be pushed forward by language towards higher-order thinking.

Lee (2011; p170) argues that meaning is 'syntactically grounded'. Therefore, internal relations are, as mentioned above, conceptual empty spaces in terms of word content, into which words are then inserted to truthfully represent/construct the world semantically. Lee uses the concepts of 'vehicle' and 'content' to describe language where 'vehicle' represents grammatical structure, which precedes 'content' representing the lexis. So externally socially referenced language can only provide semantic truth if the internal grammatical structure makes sense and is therefore internally 'true'.

We see here three layers of identity taking place; firstly, an inner one of internal rational coherence which seems common to differently constructed languages at surface level as we have seen occurring between English and Basque and English and Igala. The languages are very different at surface level yet, in the examples we have seen, there is a rational coherence through which both languages read each other in structure. Secondly, the other identity is an external one as language refers outwards to the social world in its communicative function. However, thirdly is a metalinguistic level of identity where the individual develops language as an analytical tool in examining how language itself works and later in the book – in Chapters 10 and 11 – there is considerable focus on a metalinguistic analytical identity. This becomes evident in bilingual situations where there are uncertainties in terms of how languages translate into each other, but also within discourse where texts are deconstructed for ideological meanings or other meanings ignored by the text. Again, we will examine this later in the chapters in Part Four on poststructuralism.

We are then inclined to say provisionally that different languages may well contain an internal, rational identity which is conceptually unitary and made evident in grammatical analysis between languages. Yet this cannot be an unequivocal conclusive statement because there is much research to be done across languages that are totally unrelated before we can arrive at such empirically definitive conclusions as a claim for knowledge. Walker (2019) points out that, according to Popper's concept of falsification, data such as the grammatical commonality between languages can only sustain a claim for knowledge subject to possible refutation. All knowledge can only then be temporary; in the case of empirically justifying a claim for knowledge of an underlying grammatical universality across languages even when many language grammars have been compared, such a knowledge claim can only stand until the moment where it is refuted. There may be a language or languages, yet undiscovered or unexplored, which bear no underlying grammatical relationship to those that have already been studied and their grammars classified.

Relations between structure and content

Chomsky has always insisted that the coherence of grammatical structure is independent of meaning and indeed grammatical structure contains its own meaning, irrespective of lexical meaning.

The following is an example of meaning determined by grammatical interpretation rather than lexical content:

'The duck is ready to eat' (Lee 2011; p169)

Now the surface grammar itself offers up two different meanings using the same words in the sentence. In the surface grammar the duck is either subject of the verb or object of the verb so respectively 'is ready to start eating' or 'is ready to be eaten'. The sentence syntax determines the meaning. The universal conceptualizations in this process of interpretation are still subject, verb, object but we must decide what is the agency/causation and the object of the causation in the sentence. If the 'duck' is agency then the object is a hidden category in the deep grammar, implicit in its absence and we might just say it is 'something'. If the 'duck' is the object, then there must be an agency somewhere. It is implicit but the underlying grammar would be 'ready to be eaten by someone/something'.

The simple example shows that grammar, at least at surface level, does contribute to semantics. It is, however, the Universal Grammar that offers the different possibilities, showing that we are able to conceptualize the sentence grammar or syntax extralinguistically into the categories of subject, verb, object or agency, causal action, effect, in order to elicit the different meanings.

Charlton (2014) quotes an example of a grammatical sentence that produces a nonsensical meaning solely through grammatical structure, as follows: –'Colourless green ideas sleep furiously' (2014; p63). This sticks to a subject, verb, adverbial object model and produces a meaning. It is a nonsensical meaning but that is not a contradiction in terms since it could well be a poetical meaning rather than a functional meaning. There is, however, in this sentence, a grammatical intelligibility, in the structure.

Here it is interesting to note Chomsky's (1968) reason that the above sentence can only be poetic and not a truthful reality. He claims as follows, 'We attain knowledge when inward ideas of the mind itself and the structure it creates conform to the nature of things' (Chomsky 1975; p8). So, we need more than internal unitary mental coherence. This may be enough for grammatical intelligibility, but this is only half the journey in constructing or representing the outer world through language.

Wei (2016) refers to language as a state of the faculty of human mind. He asks fundamental questions in relation to language competence. Firstly, he asks whether there is a language module in the human mind. In other words, does the metacognition and conceptualization of surface grammar in terms of UG exist within a dedicated language component of the mind or is it more generic, relating to other forms of cognition such as mathematical, spatial etc. Secondly, if UG is common to all language, at what point does it divide into separate language grammars?

Principles and parameters

McSwann (2017), along with Chomsky, posits that our own internal system of grammar establishes parameters which restrict variations, so that individual grammars do not vary to the extent that they cannot 'read' each other. The result is that although differentiated languages such as English, Russian, Spanish, etc. may vary at the surface, the underlying grammar is, in fact, undifferentiated. Wei (2016) concurs with this view that all potentialities of variation are mental and then realized in the social world.

Chomsky's view is that variation in grammar is restricted by a system of parameters, and he states as follows, 'a language is not then a system of rules but a set of specifications for parameters in an invariant system of principles of Universal Grammar' (1995b; p388).

So, UG relates to internal structures of the human mind and contains the principles of restricted variation for all languages which are parameters or settings allowing these variations to take place in surface grammar in such things as word order, case endings or position of adjectives. The criticism that can be levelled against Chomsky, as we have already mentioned, is that he does not empirically test this process across different languages to see how UG leads to surface syntactical variation in the different languages. He maintains, as follows, that 'I have not hesitated to propose a general principle of linguistic structure as the basis of observations of a single language' (Chomsky 1980b). It seems to me then that Chomsky may well be a linguistic philosopher or psychologist since he regards linguistics as a branch of human psychology, however he is perhaps not an empirical linguist who wishes to see how grammar functions in the social world within the different languages.

Chomsky seems to propose a philosophy according to which the only logically philosophical necessary condition for humans to speak a language grammatically so easily in sentences from the age of two years and to learn multiple languages also at a young age is that there is an innate structural predisposition for language in the mind. We can speak and understand sentences from this age that we have never come across before. We display creativity with language from an early age since we have not heard all the sentences we use as if we have learned them, but instead are able to formulate endless combinations of words that we have never encountered. Chomsky's notion of Poverty of Stimulus states that we do all this from very little input as we have not learned everything that we are able to express.

Therefore, because all humans use the same linguistic psychological functions with very little error, there must be a universal predisposition. Since however surface grammars do have variation there must be a principle where settings do allow limited variation in order for the universal, albeit in a limited way, to diversify into daily language practice; a limited variation since we can move between different surface linguistic grammars and yet have a good understanding of each other.

It is the task of linguists to explore the possibilities of this rational position of human identity to see how, 'on the ground', diversity comes into play; firstly, grammatical diversity and then secondly lexical/cultural diversity across languages. This diversity can really only be researched by exploring different languages and exploring the notion of UG as a conceptual metalinguistic grammar that encompasses widely varied surface grammars such as English and Basque. As explained previously, this does involve working backwards from the surface constructions to wider conceptual metacognition. This means that the term UG is perhaps no longer adequate. It needs to be defined as an extralinguistic metaprocess at work and not as any static body of knowledge.

This linguistic metaprocess as a possible framing of UG signifies flexibility in that its parameters relate to different linguistic possibilities across languages and in the use of these languages. One way of looking at language as a flexible process is through the concept of multilingualism. Kumar and Yunus (2014) attempt to reconcile formal theoretical linguistics with sociolinguistics and the way they do this is in their argument that 'human language represents a universal faculty of mind and that individual languages are simply particular examples of this faculty' (2014; p199). They, furthermore, state that 'the innate capability to learn language in a way predicts multilingualism' (2014; p208). They argue that languages are a continuum rather than each one being a hermetically sealed 'stand-alone', isolated from each other. So, consequently, because languages are porous and open to each other, linguistic competence is really a multilinguistic competence.

In order to combine this 'inner' and 'outer' as language of the universal inner capacity being able to express outer diversity, it is necessary to turn to Saussure's (1916) model of language as consisting of 'Langue' and 'Parole', where 'Langue' is the idealized mental conception of language competence and 'Parole' is how this competence is realized in social performance. So, competence is what the individual knows, and performance is the individual's language use. Chomsky echoes this himself in his later concepts of 'I' language or inner language and 'E' language or external social language.

Idealized competence or innate linguistic knowledge in relation to cultural performance can be seen reflected in the interrelation between deep and surface grammar across languages, as has been shown, when translating from an unfamiliar language. Further to this, the notion that language acquisition is a precursor to multilingualism is firstly based on the notion that linguistic borders are artificial; and consequently, secondly, porous since they all contain the same underlying grammar and therefore cannot be sealed off from each other. This latter point is exemplified in the notion of translanguaging, a process where language users employ different languages available to them as a resource in multilingual interactions. We will explore the concept and practice of translanguaging in the pedagogical section of the final chapter of the book, the Conclusion where students in multi-lingual and bilingual settings can be encouraged to move within languages as they see appropriate to express meaning.

Summary

This chapter has explored rationality as the linguistic identity of the conceptual grammar of Chomskyan Universal Grammar. I have argued for Universal Grammar as more of a process of conceptualizing grammar that is especially evident in translation where one might encounter problems with surface level word orders. Moreover, within this process there are elements of conceptual grammar that one could identify between the languages with which one has worked. Such elements include agency, action/causation, direct and indirect object. One could also add that languages should contain a means of negation, a framework for asking questions, adjectives before or after the noun, and furthermore, a means of denoting tenses with either time clauses, inflected verb endings or tonally. The list could go on because this is a matter of empirical research in classifying the world's languages. Chomsky has never done this but instead has posited that which must be logically necessary for us to learn a language and for it to be intelligible internally and to each other.

I would like to consider the possible conclusions of this chapter for identity in terms of sameness and difference and how this may well relate to the ensuing chapters.

Conclusion

I have argued that Universal Grammar is a process of conceptualization as a metacognition that exists outside language, but which can be expressed within language by such terms as agency, intentionality, causation, action, time, object or effect of action. These terms are conceptual ones which could be used for other areas of mental life, but they can relate to language. They are necessary concepts which seem necessary for a sentence to be internally intelligible and, as already stated, a sentence or an utterance cannot index an external reality unless it has an internal coherence.

I have empirically demonstrated that the conceptualization mentioned above relates to two completely unrelated European languages, English and Basque.

This conclusion as a claim for general truth is not incontrovertible because it would need to be corroborated across all the languages of the world if it is going to have generalizable empirical validation. There may be in existence a language or languages which operate, somehow, differently and as Popper (1994) points out knowledge can at any moment be falsifiable, thereby always remaining provisional until proved otherwise.

Nevertheless, with UG there is a notion of sameness which allows for variation through the principle of parameters. If there were no principle of parameters, we would all read and speak the same surface grammar. The parameters allow for difference in the area where grammar interacts with culture and, and at this level, cultural forces act to shape grammar where parameters permit this. It is interesting that we can trace these surface cultural grammars back to the universal concepts such as agency, causality, action, object/effect.

Grammar relates to identity then at the different levels. UG reflects a human unitary rationality located in our mental structures and which then is expressed culturally in different grammars reflecting a more diverse identity. These two facets of identity therefore relate to mind and culture expressing both sameness and difference, respectively. We could then argue that humans are structurally the same in terms of mind but different in terms of culture. The parameters principle seems to provide an explanation showing how mind diversifies into culture and then onwards where cultural difference proliferates through lexicogrammar, lexis and language as a social practice. In turn this culture acts back to shape lexicogrammar in a language–culture dialectic

Cultural grammar differences must, nevertheless, be limited so that we can understand one another, however imperfectly, across languages and, as language moves from culture to culture and within cultures, more and more differences occur where words both represent and construct different meanings which often cannot be translated with exactitude.

Language, then, moves through UG, principles of parameters, multilingual UG and variations in grammar with a direction of travel from sameness to difference. It is, therefore, sameness which provides the foundation for the differences to come.

2

Cognition, Knowledge and Identity in Language

This chapter extends the view of grammar and rational identity to the rest of language by focusing firstly on propositions of truth, what we can know through language, and secondly on conceptualization and cognition.

The first part of the chapter has a focus on understanding and logic within language and does this by looking at how statements and propositions can form a picture of the world within language.

The second part of the chapter moves identity away from language itself towards the non-linguistic in relation to the linguistic. The area of cognitive linguistics, within this relationship, focuses on non-linguistic features of mind such as imagery, spatial conceptualization and metaphor.

Wittgenstein's view of language

The first part of this chapter explores Wittgenstein's view of reality which was that everything we purport to know is contained within language. The first and last statements in his Tractatus Logico-Philosophicus (1999) are as follows, firstly in the preface, 'What can be said at all can be said clearly; and whereof one cannot speak thereof one must be silent' and lastly in statement number 7, his final statement is to reiterate as follows, 'Whereof one cannot speak, thereof one must be silent'. He furthermore states in the preface that 'The limit to thinking can only be drawn in language and what is on the other side of the limit will simply be nonsense.'

We will see in the second part of the chapter how this stands in stark contrast with Cognitive Linguistics which seeks to draw parallels between linguistic phenomena and the non-linguistic world of images and metaphor where language is drawn out of imagery. We shall also see in Chapter 6 how Wittgenstein's view of language does not correspond to Austin's (Longworth 2011) view of performative linguistics which, as illocutionary speech acts, do not need of necessity to bear a description of the world, but simply a shared understanding practically and functionally as to what words mean.

However, in Wittgenstein's work in the Tractatus as well as in his later work, he states that the limits of language are the limits of the known world and, by extension, identity is firmly placed within language. Meanings are worked out within language in propositions which form a picture of reality as it is; in the Tractatus the foundation for this is the word-object intrinsic alignment. We can see his point of departure in statement number 2 of the Tractatus stating as follows:

'What is the case, the fact is the existence of atomic facts'.

and, in statement 2.01,

'An atomic fact is a combination of objects (entities and things)'.

Basic truths then exist at the smallest scale of language where word and object lie in a one-to one relationship. From this 'atomic' beginning a picture is built up which forms a picture of the world. In Tractatus 2.1 he says,

'We make ourselves pictures of facts'

and in 2.12

'The picture is a model of reality'.

We will see, later in our exploration of Cognitive Linguistics, that pictures are conceptualized as non-linguistic within mind and called forward by language whereas in Wittgenstein the picture of the world and therefore our understanding is totally within language. In 2.13 Wittgenstein states 'To the objects correspond in the picture, the elements of the picture'. He closely aligns a tight fit between propositions being a picture of the world and the world by saying in 2.16 'In order to be a picture a fact must have something in common with what it pictures' and in 2.161 'In the picture and the pictured there must be something identical in order to know that the one can be a picture of the other at all'. So, language, as we use it, to be any good, must be, by this account, a very similar picture of reality. Otherwise, we would just speak nonsense.

Wittgenstein however does not say there is an absolute total fit between language and total reality, as opposed to reality as we know it, because he accepts that there may be a world outside of the known world, only the latter of which is covered by language; however, we can never know the former because as we have already seen in statement number 7, we cannot speak of it. What we cannot speak of, we cannot know.

This must surely remind us of Kant in the Critique of Pure Reason (1993) where reality is that which is presented to us, not in language as in Wittgenstein, but in the case of Kant, perception. The similarity in Kant lies in the perception-reality alignment whereas in Wittgenstein it is the language-reality alignment. This leaves room for something, which Kant calls the 'Noumenon' which is not covered by either by perception or by language. In 6.522 of the Tractatus Wittgenstein says, 'There is indeed the inexpressible. This shows itself; it is the mystical'.

Rational identity of language

Wittgenstein builds up the rational identity of language starting from object-word which he calls 'atomic facts' and these form an internal logic as he states, 'In logic nothing is accidental; if a thing can occur in an atomic fact, the possibility of that atomic fact must already be prejudged in the thing'.

We can see that the statement above is an analytical truth of internal logic where 'the thing' is in the 'atomic fact' and the 'atomic fact' is prejudged in 'the thing'. This makes 'the thing' and the 'atomic fact' interchangeable since both subject and object are the same. Because of the one-to-one fit between the thing and the word, Wittgenstein says in 3.032 'To present in language anything which contradicts logic is as impossible as in geometry to present by its coordinates a figure which contradicts the laws of space'. Consequently, the elementary propositions which are the atomic facts containing word-object correspondence contain an analytical truth. This is a tautology in which subject and predicate are the same in such a statement as 'All men are male', or 'All creatures are mortal therefore man is mortal' where to be one is also to be the other. Kant would have presented this as an a priori truth, as an elementary proposition. The above statements would then be analytical a priori statements of which the purpose in terms of identity is to state an intrinsic and absolute truth proposition where the object is contained in the subject. We do not learn anything new as we would in a synthetic proposition where something new is introduced when the object of the statement is different from the subject of the statement. Wittgenstein's statements as pictures of the world are synthetic in that to say something new, subject and object of a statement must be different, although to be true, they must point to the same picture of the world.

Based on this Wittgenstein establishes complex propositions which form a true picture of the world, but which are non-analytical as it attempts to say something of the world. An analytical truth says nothing of the world because subject and predicate are identical. However, a proposition proposes a statement to constitute a picture of the world where subject and predicate are not the same and which Kant would call a synthetic truth. Ahmed (2011) claims Wittgenstein's position was that 'every non-elementary proposition is a truth function of elementary ones' (2011; p81 – Philosophy of Language: Lee (ed.)).

Wittgenstein himself says in statement 5 of the Tractatus, 'Propositions are truth functions of elementary propositions.' From an external perspective the truth proposition must form a verbal picture of reality. The atomic facts-words must be arranged to form a picture which corresponds to reality. As Ahmed argues, 'Hence to account for the truth-grounds of a proposition is to account for its content' (2011; p81).

The analytical truth of the elementary proposition does not say anything about the world beyond an internal self-evident truth. However, an external truth proposition makes a claim about the world where, as already mentioned, subject and object are different. To contrast with the last chapter on Chomsky where rationality was contained in grammar yet devoid of meaning, Wittgenstein proposes rational statements about the world based on truth propositions of meaning. Rationality then has moved outwards from internal grammatical relations as in Chomsky towards propositional relations based on internal logic, and then projected externally out into the world in terms of meaning.

Therefore, for a proposition to have a true meaning, beyond internal relations of logic, it must express something external to itself. Macha (2015) claims that for a truthful proposition 'the symbolising fact and the symbolized fact have to be in accordance' (2015; p49). Macha furthermore argues that 'It is obvious that the comparison between language and pictures lies at the heart of the Tractatus' (2011; p67).

To sum up, the language narrative is hierarchical as follows, 'An elementary proposition consists of names. A proposition is a truth-function of elementary propositions. Language is the totality of all propositions' (2011; p69 – quoted from the Tractatus). At the base of the hierarchy are the elementary atomic facts-word-objects which are independent analytical truths, and which can combine with others to form mutually dependent combinations in the proposition. The verification of the proposition is externally facing in a comparison with a reality picture of the world.

Wittgenstein's later philosophy of language

Wittgenstein develops a more comprehensive view of language in his later work 'Philosophical Investigations' (2009). More 'comprehensive' in the way he defines word meanings by encompassing the way a word is used in social contexts or as he calls them 'language games.' In this respect Wittgenstein's view becomes more sociological rather than philosophical. He comes to acknowledge, as many linguists have from other paradigms, that the word has no philosophical absolute grounding, and its identity is shaped in the way it is currently being used. Word meanings then depend on social life and can change of course from one social language game to another.

At the beginning of Philosophical Investigations (2009), Wittgenstein quotes St Augustine's view of language which is a word to object naming of the world, and of course this model of meaning is at the root of the Tractatus.

However, Wittgenstein questions who should decide what a word means, which is a question of linguistic identity. Should this be a group of influential people who, for example, create dictionaries or other language authorities who decide that this word means this, and that word means that? Furthermore, how do you explain a word if not by the use of other words since, without an ultimate authority, there is no absolute standard finalizing a judgement on meaning? Some countries such as France have Academies which preside over the language of the nation and make judgements on correct usage. However, this is arbitrary and can only be carried by social power. Therefore, in the final analysis one explains symbols through the use of other symbols and there is no ultimate grounding of meaning and therefore identity.

The conclusion of this is that one cannot explain what words mean, one can only demonstrate their wide variety of meanings in different situations or as Wittgenstein states, 'Language Games'. Philosophical Investigations explores language games and gives lots of examples of how word meanings change in different contexts. One of the examples given in the book is the use of the word 'Slab'. Now we could all agree in the context of a builder's yard that 'Slab' means a fairly large block of concrete and by agreement this would be its referential use. However, the word used in action on a building site might mean something different. If then a builder is calling out to another builder 'Slab', he is likely to really mean 'Pass me the slab' as he is using the word in an elliptical manner. Therefore, this word used elliptically might mean a whole sentence rather than just referentially and this is precisely an example of how word meanings can change or, in this case, expand according to use. Another example is the grammatical question 'Isn't the weather glorious?'. Strictly speaking this is a grammatical question but when spoken in context becomes a rhetorical statement. This could even be an expression of sarcasm if the weather is exactly the opposite of glorious!

Meanings are not just a question of the words as graphemes but also as phonemes in tones of voice. In a certain situation I could say, 'That's just marvellous isn't it?'. However, the meaning of this depends on the context and the tone of voice. This could be a reaction to a situation which has gone horribly wrong and consequently uttered in sarcasm, as well as a literal joyful response to a positive situation.

Wittgenstein in Philosophical Investigations (2009) statement number 23 states that language becomes a 'form of life'. In this statement he gives examples of these language games or forms of life as follows, 'Giving orders and obeying them; Describing the appearances of an object or giving its measurement; Constructing an object from a description (drawing); Reporting an event; Speculating about an event'.

Wittgenstein also calls into question the identity of objects in using them as a grounding for word identity since objects are complex rather than elementary. A chair for example is made up of its parts to make a chair and these are made up of wood which is in turn made up of molecules and then of atoms and so, although words might be constructions from phonemes, the objects themselves are also constructions. So, a word which has no essence is erroneously aligned to an object which has no substantial essence, therefore a matching up of entities without grounded essences. Consequently, one cannot explain a word, either in terms of another word, nor in terms of a matching object but one can only show the use of a word in its many language games.

In moving from non-grounded attempts at essentialist word explanations to showing the use of words in context, the linguistics or philosophy of language is moving from linguistic essential identity to an existential identity. In this move to an existential identity, we understand that word meanings are never completed and can always have fresh definitions in fresh situations. There is a parallel for this in individual personal identity which in existential terms would be unbounded and always free in definition and action.

We see in this book the recurring and central theme of language and identity as both Sameness and Difference, and the work of Wittgenstein in the Tractatus and Philosophical Investigations encapsulates both sameness and difference, respectively.

Logic

If the essence of words is unavailable, where is the logic of language because, much like in the work of Saussure in a different linguistic tradition, the internal logic between 'signifier' and 'signified' has been broken. Nevertheless, Wittgenstein maintains that 'There must be order in the vaguest sentence' (Philosophical Investigations statement 98). Order is still maintained in the fit between language and the world, therefore in language propositions that constitute a picture of the world. However instead of explaining and defining words in isolation as we find in the Tractatus, we now describe the use of language in its context. In statement 120 of Philosophical Investigations Wittgenstein claims as follows: 'When I talk about language (words, sentences etc.) I must speak the language of everyday', since philosophy cannot give language its foundation, it can only describe language in its use.

For Wittgenstein there is in philosophy as in language nothing hidden from view. There are no deep mystical meanings in language or philosophy. Everything is visible but just needs clarification and for Wittgenstein philosophy does not create meanings, it clarifies them. Similarly, language does not construct meanings from nowhere; it is a tool for an accurate description of the world as it exists. At any given moment, all identity is present. It may be developing but it will be visible and verifiable as it does so, but nonetheless, ever present. Let us not forget that Wittgenstein, in point 7 of the Tractatus, says that outside of language there is nonsense – it is something we cannot rationally speak of. For Wittgenstein philosophy is an activity and has no content; it is simply, like language, an act of clarification.

Logic then is in the primacy of the word in which its propositions, when combined together, have to make sense by offering up a description of the world and not an explanation.

Beyond words, nothing can be said. This does not mean that there is nothing; but beyond words, nothing cannot be spoken of and so, unlike Cognitive Linguistics which we will explore in the second half of the chapter, there is nothing non-linguistic which has any meaning.

Wittgenstein's use of grammar, unlike Chomsky who refers to deep levels of logic, permeates across language rather than underneath it. So, grammar is in the combination of words that make an intelligible proposition about the world. Unlike Chomsky who divorces rationality from meaning in grammar, Wittgenstein's grammar is the order and rationality of meaning in language. Wittgenstein would not offer explanations of grammar because there is nothing to explain because in turn there is nothing hidden from view. One describes the world in all its language games and then when nothing else can be described (not explained) one falls silent.

Many might feel that Wittgenstein's philosophy of language is flat. It might travel widely into different contexts, but it has no depth and does not call upon the non-linguistic world. In some respects, Wittgenstein resembles the post-structuralists of Foucault and Derrida who maintain that outside language or text there is nothing; except to note that for Wittgenstein the text really is language as words whereas for Derrida, the text is everything semiotic in the world. For Foucault the world is constructed through language and discourse and can only be seen through this prism, so there is no neutral world outside of language. We can see then the centrality of language and semiotics in both the analytical philosophical tradition which is elucidation and description and also the Continental philosophical tradition. Nevertheless, there are other branches of linguistics that do draw upon non-linguistic features of understanding and identity such as externally facing social structures and internally facing conceptual structures.

Since the general progression of this book is to move outwards from the original departure point of grammar as a core rationality, it is opportune now, in the second section of this chapter, to move to the relationship between language and the non-linguistic areas of mind as proposed by cognitive linguistics. This moves us away from just language as proposed by Chomsky and Wittgenstein to suggest that other areas outside of language come into play in their relationship with language.

The cognitive turn

In this section we move from identity contained within language to a wider view of identity involving non-linguistic areas of individuals within mental structures.

Cognitive linguistics draws upon conceptual development which is separate from language and yet related to it, in that it feeds into language and in turn reciprocally draws upon language. Jackendoff (2007) separates conceptual thought from phonetic patterns so that the development of language is about mapping concepts and thoughts onto sound patterns. In this model then, language involves cognitive organization as humans have developed the ability to turn thoughts into sounds by organizing them in words as well as drawing thoughts out of words. Jackendoff separates phonemes from conceptual thought as being distinct and yet, in social contact, the phonemes come to be populated by thoughts to form words. Vygotsky, in *Thought and Language* (1986), performs a similar operation when he states that sound patterns and thought come from different mental sources and then join together in early childhood, when the associations take place between the two phenomena. Consequently, it can be argued that the phoneme is a physical sound which, in very early childhood, is empty of meaning beyond instinctual noise until it is associated with meaning through social contact in a meaning making environment.

Jackendoff argues for linear grammar as a mental grammar to transfer thoughts and concepts into sound patterns, but this is only a starting point in the development of language. Linear grammar depends upon word order and suggests that a simple word order grammar is a feature of the human brain, although not as a language isolated module as in Chomskyan linguistics.

Jackendoff (2007 in the Linguistics Review) argues that linguistic capacity is layered as follows:

1. The essential components are conceptual structures, phonology and linear order. This would constitute a very basic protolanguage.
2. Refinements are syntactic categories, phrase structures and inflectional morphology in recursive grammar.

Consequently, in evolutionary terms number two is founded upon the essential components of number one.

The salient characteristic in this schema is that, in the essential first layer of linguistic capacity, there exists a non-linguistic conceptual structure, which becomes translated into language through linear order grammar. Linear order grammar however is a basic language without recursive grammar where word and image are matched one for one and so the grammar is based on word order rather than on syntax. Jackendoff (2007) argues that there are some pidgin languages spoken in the world which have not developed beyond basic linear word order grammar. This means that one could not have sentences with relative clauses which defy natural conceptual word order, such as for example: 'The man to whom I sold the car had grey hair'. Here, within this sentence there are two sentences and combining them into one sentence with a relative subordinate clause is a feature of recursive grammar. Within a more basic language of linear grammar, one would need to express the meanings in two sentences as follows: 1- I sold the car to the man. 2- The man had grey hair. Recursive grammar would easily allow for another clause to be added creating another sentence as follows, 'I told you a story about the man, to whom I sold the car who had grey hair,' and one could even add another subordinate clause as follows, 'I told you a story about the man, to whom I sold the car who had grey hair who was about to go on holiday'. There are four linear grammatical sentences in this recursive grammatical sentence with its three relative clauses which are as follows: 1- I told you the story about the man; 2- I sold the car to the man; 3- The man had grey hair; 4- The man was about to go on holiday. Recursiveness in grammar allows for creativity and, in a rewording of this latter sentence to create an even further distance from linear grammar, one could have as follows: 'The man who had grey hair to whom I sold the car, whose story I told, was about to go on holiday'. Such creativity liberates language from its one-to-one grounding in terms of linear word-object relations. The 'man' is still the subject of the one sentence with four relative clauses as predicates which in linear grammar would require four separate sentences.

Recursive grammar then interposes syntax between the basic conceptual structure, on which linear grammar is based, and phonology so that such complex sentences can be vocalized.

Jackendoff (2007) maintains that linear conceptual structure is a feature of mind in the formation of this layered language, as follows:

1 Protolanguage – linear word order in line with basic cognition
2 More elaborate surface syntactical structure.

This demonstrates how cognitive linguistics has emerged from Chomskyan generative formal linguistics in terms of the layering; linear grammar consequently aligns with Universal Grammar and a subsequent more developed surface grammar constitutes the individual languages. The big difference that exists between Chomsky and Jackendoff is that cognitive linguistics of which Jackendoff is one of the founders draws heavily on semantics. Meaning is an integral part of the basic linear grammar which in turn is a grammar lodged in mental structures.

Basic meaning or semantic structure originates in the conceptual structure and the conceptual structure stands alongside syntax and phonology where all three rest on equal footing as the three pillars of Jackendoff's Parallel Architecture. Here there is no specific modular approach as in formal linguistics where language develops in isolation from the rest of mental structures. In cognitive linguistics, language is a feature of cognition in the same way as spatial structure and perception. In this way there are mental structures that interrelate with language, but which do not depend upon language because in evolutionary terms they existed prior to language. There would be therefore an interface between areas of conceptual structures such as imagery and spatial structures prior to language. Cognitive linguistics would consider these areas as non-linguistic areas of the mind which nonetheless interrelate with language.

A fundamental question that arises is that if these conceptual structures are non-linguistic, in what do they consist? How is the rest of mind constituted, if one claims that there are characteristics, relating to language, which are distinctly non-linguistic?

Certain features come to mind which are such things as imagery, metaphor, spatial concepts of distance and depth, causality and more generally the notions of will and intentionality. In the latter case for example, if one wills something to happen, can one say that this is a linguistic event? Similarly, if one sees an image, let us say a cloud pattern of a dog, can one understand the image for what it is without translating it into the word 'dog'? In the latter case, this is not unequivocal because a young child may already have conceptualized 'dog' along with the word. One could at least claim then that the image evokes the concept constructed through the word. In this sense the meaning resides with the image as well as with the word and indeed both become signs.

Jackendoff (2007) refers to language as a combination of mental faculties which serve other purposes besides language. He quotes Wilkins (2005; p273) as follows, 'We do not know a priori which features of the cognitive system are necessarily language specific'. However, it may be that language cuts across all areas of cognition and moreover Hart (2014) argues that the conceptual system, as a whole, is based on image structures and that language draws upon these structures. He claims as follows ' – grammar encodes a simulated visuo-spatial experience' – (2014; p135). Furthermore, these visualizations can encode ideological meanings as he claims, 'Visuo-spatial experience is at the root of conceptualization' – (2014; p136).

Hart furthermore claims that the cognitive system is not just based upon structural images but also upon metaphorical images which are ideological and which through grammar enact ideology. We will explore this connection in the next chapter.

Two main paradigms of Cognitive Linguistics

Schwartz-Friesel (2012) argues that the subject area of Cognitive Linguistics is at war with itself due to a split with regard to its relationship with mind. She explains that cognitive linguistics emerged from the formal linguistics of generative grammar because there was no longer an acceptance by some linguists that there was a specific language module in the brain, as in fact Chomsky had argued. Linguists such as Lakoff (1987) and Langacker (1987, 1999) advanced the view that the language facility, as an innate quality in the mind, is a conceptual structure alongside and parallel to other non-linguistic conceptual areas and that there is an interrelationship between the linguistic and non-linguistic areas.

There are however other cognitive linguists who maintain the Chomskyan belief that the linguistic area of the brain is modular. Schwarz-Friesel (2012) argues for a middle position stating that language is a cognitive system interrelating with other non-linguistic cognitive systems but that it is indeed modular to some extent. She makes this claim because of the evidence of language aphasia where, due to pathology, there has been loss of linguistic ability and yet evidence of cognitive abilities remaining intact. This, then, argues for at least some separation between cognition and language. She does not make clear, however, how, outside of language and sign, such general cognitive facilities were tested.

As mentioned in this chapter, and in a different linguistic tradition, Vygotsky (1986) claims that language and thought do indeed originate from different places in the mind but then come together in early childhood, where instinctive phonemes which had been simply imitated by the child become associated with meanings in the social world mediated by a conceptual system. It would seem reasonable to assert that the phonological system and the conceptual-cognitive system do come together at some stage. As Vygotsky claims in his tradition of language-thought, language subsequently generates higher-order thinking and, as we have just seen in the previous section, it is able to do this due to the creativity of recursive grammar. Although I believe this to be a reasonable assertion, it needs to be underpinned by empirical evidence, thereby connecting higher-order abstract thinking to syntax.

Schwartz-Friesel (2012) argues that the notion of an interaction between language and non-linguistic cognition makes cognitive linguistics an intrinsically multidisciplinary area of study and research. Consequently, she criticizes the subject area for not collecting sufficient empirical data and for relying too much on philosophical introspection. She proposes that '——the integration between empirical and theoretical approaches, the expansion of methods and the application of data from interdisciplinary cognition research should be the main goal of future research' (2012; pp656–64, Language Sciences 34).

Imagery and metaphor as cognition

It has been argued that images often underpin language, and we witness young children representing the world in drawing and painting. Furthermore, teaching methods at infant and primary schools rely on visual presentation and the relationship between images and indeed this is still the case in the first few years of secondary school. Learning becomes more abstract, and word based in the more senior Key Stages 4 and 5 in secondary schools. That visual display in images forms a large part of cognition in early years' development so that the complexity of words, sentences and grammar are bypassed seems to me to be a 'given' and surely acknowledged by anyone who has children in infant or primary school education. Furthermore, we learn about the world before the world is put into words, perhaps through gesture or facial expression or tone of voice. Language mediates a world which pre-exists the individual and comes on top of interrelating images and non-verbal communication of gestures and emotional context. It is possible for individuals to have understandings of the world before they can even represent it back to themselves and to others in language. Langacker (1987) who is one of the founding fathers of cognitive linguistics holds that cognitive and organizational patterns in language reveal existing patterns in mind and so cognitive linguistics is a path to understanding the mind.

In this we can see how identity has moved from language itself in Wittgenstein to the individual in terms of his or her non-linguistic mental contents in relation to language.

The connection between language and conceptual structures, according to Bosman (2019), is through metaphor which connects mental contents to language through imagery. Bosman furthermore claims that one of the stepping stones on the way between the word and the image metaphor is metonymy. Metonymy is where a word stands in place of another of which the former is a part of a larger word image. For example, a political comment on a news item might read as follows, 'Number 10 refutes any claims of wrong-doing in the financial scandal'. Now how can a number 10 or any number undertake a political action? The number has to refer to something bigger than the materiality of the word grapheme. Of course, it does by referring to the residence of the UK prime minister which in turn refers to the institute of government. Another political example could be as follows: –'Washington would like to start peace talks with the Taliban'. Again, how could a city engage in diplomatic discourse? The word then means more than its place name and indeed means the government of the United States of America. So, a word calls into action a much larger image than is materially contained in the grapheme or the phoneme of the word itself. This therefore draws upon a larger image within the mind of the reader or listener. The word, as a result, relies on the connection to the image and moreover when the word is completely unrelated to the image in its normal discourse and yet still connected in the evocation of an image, this is a metaphor. Therefore, a word evoking an image from a different discourse than the word itself would be classed as a metaphor.

Bosman (2019) uses religious images to illustrate this metaphorical use of language in the Christian faith. She argues that Christian imagery is replete with examples of imagery connected to language such as 'Lamb of God' in referring to Jesus Christ. This is a metaphor because it does not refer, in its principle, to a physical woolly creature but rather directly to innocence and sacrifice. As Bosman argues, for metaphorical image references to work, the reader needs to know the culture and even the history of the culture where such a reference is employed. Here the nature of the cultural reference is a religious one where one needs to know that in the Old Testament animals were used in sacrifice to gain atonement for sins. One then needs to know that the lamb is regarded as the epitome of innocence and that in the Christian faith, this personifies Jesus who is then the innocent sacrifice for the atonement of human sin. Even someone who is brought up in Western culture but not in a Christian culture might not understand this metaphor and therefore not understand why a woolly creature is connected to God. So, although language is connected to imagery and metaphors populate words, not everyone understands culturally specific metaphors. We can see then in cognitive linguistics that conceptual and spatial structures in the mind are translated into images and then through the lexicon and syntactical structures, metaphors are created.

So, a metaphor carries a meaning through an image which, in physical terms of the graphemes, does not make sense and especially to someone who is not attuned to the particular culture. In footballing discourse, how often does one hear a commentator excitedly shouting 'The ball has just hit the woodwork'. If one does not know football nor its discourse one might be puzzled by 'woodwork', because nowadays on a football field there is no wood to hit inside the field of play. Of course, this is a direct metaphor for the goals as the posts in history would have been made of wood. So, this image of woodwork which to the uninitiated could mean a wooden construction evokes the goal even though the physical phoneme/grapheme bears no resemblance to a goal. Words are then more than the most basic physical common meaning would signify and they can become populated with images which do not align with the basic signification. There is then the possibility of a word image identity mismatch if one does not understand the culture. This takes identity away from words in the Chomsky-Wittgenstein sense and places it inside the interplay between word, image and culture, with culture playing a crucial part in identity construction.

Lakoff (2012) takes the notion of imagery and metaphor as originating in embodiment. For example, he represents verbs of motion as originating in our own bodies, based upon our physical experiences such as running. So, we understand 'to run' because we have experience of this ourselves. Lakoff claims, 'The concepts for what the physical body is and does are embodied' (2012; p775). Lakoff argues that conceptual structures organize visual perception, motor action, spatial relations and mental images and these form a natural language. He refers to them as universal cognitive structures which are common to everyone as 'cognitive primitives' (2012; p775). Metaphors are conceptual and originate from cognitive primitives which rise to the surface in language. Although metaphors are abstract as a blend of image and language, Lakoff regards them as embodied within the brain and so if we refer to the visuospatial conceptual phenomena as the non-linguistic areas of mind, we can again see the expansion of notions of identity moving away from uniquely being couched in language and rationality. Identity is then both linguistic and non-linguistic not as separate binary items but as interrelated.

Conclusion

We can see that a word takes on meanings far beyond its every day physical significance, demonstrating that the identity of a word does not always rest with the word itself but with an image or a metaphorical concept. In pedagogy, before students know a word it might need to be explained to them in a diagram. An example of this might be the word 'dialectic'. This word could be understood in the context of other words which 'scaffold' its meaning. However, in a teaching situation it might be more easily explained in a small diagram with parallel arrowed lines in the same direction and a forward moving spiral in between them, showing two elements which influence each other and in doing so cause change in each of the elements. The two changed elements then continue to influence each other resulting in more change and so on perhaps 'ad infinitum'. The changed elements in the forward pointing parallel lines could be shaded more intensely as each change occurs. A labelled diagram would perhaps show this more readily and, subsequently, when a student uses the word, s/he may well evoke the word's image alongside the word itself.

An interesting question to consider at the end of this chapter is to ask if all conceptual relationships can be reduced to diagrams or mind maps? This might be the case for teaching but not for practical use of words which need to respond to and construct quick moving life situations. The image eventually becomes encompassed within the use of the word, in its efficient everyday usage.

The notion of identity in language takes on a much wider perspective in cognitive linguistics than in the linguistic philosophy of Wittgenstein because it involves human beings themselves rather than the disembodied language of Wittgenstein and Chomsky. Wittgenstein, in his later work, does acknowledge word meanings being determined by social situations in his 'language games' and he does refer to language use, but he does not involve the mind of the human being and how it might be constituted. He sticks with language rather than the human user and his/her mental content. On the other hand, cognitive linguistics takes on a wider view of meaning-making in terms of the non-linguistic world.

We see a much more complete picture of language in cognitive linguistics where identity is manifested in language through its interrelationship with other areas of mind and furthermore as, Lakoff argues, embodiment. Because language, in terms of words and sentences, is only one feature of the mind, one needs an expansion into non-linguistic areas such as gesture and tone of voice which bypass syntax but which are still generated by mind and conceptual structure.

Within language itself in terms of words and sentences we also see how language and identity ascend to a higher order of thought through the recursiveness of syntax where meaning becomes more and more refined but at the same time takes up less space. The semantics are more spatially compact in language through relative subordinate clauses. This creates a density of language where, through relative adjectives, relative pronouns and subordinate clauses, more meanings are generated with fewer lexical items. In this process one can see that there is not a division between grammar and lexis but a relationship between them connected by the meaning-making nature of language use and interpretation. Relative adjectives and relative pronouns for example are features of recursive grammar making for more complex sentences and yet at the same time are integral to the semantics of the language as opposed to being just mechanistic features.

Notions of identity therefore in this chapter have broadened horizontally into non-linguistic areas of life and, also linguistically have developed more vertically into higher-order thinking through the complexity of recursive grammatical constructions.

The progressive rationale of this book is to explore a burgeoning development in linguistic and personal identities as we see language expanding its frontiers from its core internal relations of rational grammar and truth propositions to encompass more externally facing aspects of the non-linguistic world.

In the chapters of the next part, we see language and identity moving outwards in a more interpretive way in relations with social structures.

Part Two

Grammar and Cultural Identity

3

Systemic Functional Grammar

Introduction

The outwardly progressing trajectory of Language and Identity has journeyed from a static state of innate rational grammar and rational language of truth propositions towards an increasingly external referential view of language. In the previous chapter we had referred to word–object connection and phrase and sentence connection with external reality to substantiate a truth proposition. We had also referred beyond words and sentences to include metaphor and images within mental structures as contributing to the construction of language. In these language paradigms of Part One, identity of language was a matter of the mind either as rational grammar, mental–external world truth propositions or the metaphors and images of the mind.

In this part we move away from mental structures into the area of social structures in the construction of language, grammar and concomitant identity. One question to ask and hopefully answer is the extent to which social structures are represented within mental structures. Is there a dividing line between what is mind and furthermore individual mind and what is social space or do the two areas overlap at some point? So, do we talk about mind as being social or is it still individualized?

Halliday

Halliday (2002) criticizes formal linguistics for its exclusive focus on inner structures in its explanation of language without any recourse to social structures. This is a point for debate considering that linguistic explanations may be divided and unresolved over whether humans have innate mental structures or whether they are primarily social beings. Vygotsky (1986) maintains that humans are social before they become individual. So, the linguistic divide in terms of identity may reflect the wider philosophical divide in identity between individual and social. As previously mentioned, philosophically this is represented by the difference between, on the one hand, Descartes' notion of individual mind and innate mental structures and, on the other, Locke's view of mind as social.

Even Locke (2010-15), however, acknowledged that there had to be some inherent human capacity for learning to take place at all, to provide some sort of mental platform to receive the external world.

Exploring language and individual mind, consequently, focuses on what makes language intelligible at all. Even if it were admitted that language is a social phenomenon, what are the mental structures that render it intelligible to the individual? Part One, which looked at language from the inside, concluded that there is an intelligibility at the core of language which corresponds with features of mind. Chomsky argues for an innate language module as Universal Grammar whereas the counter argument, underpinned by the philosophy of Locke, is for a social mind characterized by an ability to learn. So, the latter argument is simply that mind is an ability to learn and otherwise, prior to the social world, it is of itself a 'blank slate'.

Halliday's systemic functional language is concerned with 'freeing grammar from the restrictions imposed by structures' (2002; p12). For Halliday, grammar is not contained in the closed circuit of the mind, but rather represents and even constructs the social world. For Halliday, Chomsky's renowned intelligible grammatical sentence 'Colorless green ideas sleep furiously' makes no sense at all because it cannot represent the external world in any functional way. For Chomsky this sentence is acceptable because it has all the rational grammatical components for intelligibility – it has a subject followed by a verb and an adverbial predicate and although it makes no functional sense because of the obvious contradiction in terms between 'colorless' and 'green', it could be argued that it makes poetical sense. Chomskyan grammar has, consequently, internal rationality in structure but does not pretend to have social meaning whereas Halliday's SFL grammar is closely tied to the functionality of the social world. So, we have an inner mental grammar and an outer social grammar, and as we move from language as rational understanding to language as social communication respectively, we move from language in itself to language use. This means a move towards individual and social use of language and with this, the discipline of sociolinguistics focusing on linguistic practice as opposed to inner structures. This dichotomy between language as inner rationality on the one hand and, on the other, language as external social communication is reflected in this book title *Language and Identity: Rationality and Interpretation*. As we focus on language in the social world, our focus shifts towards language use and the user, in terms of his/her interpretation of the world through language.

Halliday, in referring to the dichotomous development of formal linguistics and applied linguistics, deplores 'this split between two aspects of what to me is a single enterprise, that of trying to explain language. It seems to me however that both parts of the project are weakened where they are divided one from the other' (2002; p10). Halliday furthermore claims that outside of institutional specialisms 'no very clear line is drawn between linguistics and applied linguistics'.

In defence of such a split, it can be argued that the greater the focus on a subject area, the greater the chance of subdivisions as focus becomes more detailed, less general and therefore more specialist. We now have so many branches of linguistics such as pragmatics, semantics, historical, forensic, psycholinguistics, sociolinguistics, stylistics, discourse analysis, etc. but they should be able to complement each other rather than be at war under the opposing banners of formal and applied linguistics.

Systemic functional grammar

Halliday (2002) differentiates between grammar and lexis. However, he argues that this distinction is not an abrupt one but rather a continuum between grammar as a 'closed system' (2000; p40) and lexis as 'open set patterns in language' (2000; p41). Halliday acknowledges the contribution made by Chomsky in the notion of the stratification of grammar. Grammatical items therefore have deep level structure in holding lexis together, providing semantic direction and externally facing relations. Halliday claims as follows that 'underlying grammar is semantically significant grammar' (2002; p112). He defines underlying grammar as an 'abstract representation of grammatical relations and syntactic organization' (2002; p106).

If, as an example of the underlying grammatical coherence of surface grammar, we take subject pronouns such as 'he/she/ it' or 'they' into consideration, we can see that at a structural level the subject pronouns represent the mental concept of agency in denoting who or what is generating an action such as in the sentence 'She/he speaks the truth'. At the same time, at surface level, this grammatical item designates the social category of gender. Furthermore, this underlying strategic level of grammatical agency, at the same time, designates at the surface in French and Spanish both gender and number in 'Ils/Elles' and 'Ellos/Ellas', respectively. This means that grammatical items can simultaneously have two levels of operation, one underlying and strategic in agency and one descriptive in social category. In this case there is some answer to the previously stated question as to whether or not there is a dividing line between mental structures and social structures to the extent that there are grammatical situations, as mentioned above, in which both are simultaneously called into play.

Halliday proposes, however, that language/grammar starts with meaning rather than rational mechanisms so that, as a result, grammatical arrangements are constructed socially to express meaning rather than as emanating impersonally from rational grammatical form. Language is therefore led by semantics and meaning arises from the interaction between linguistic items and the material world. Therefore, the lexis–grammar continuum emerges out of a semantic interaction with the social world. The mental question however has to remain in terms of the inner rational platform on which socially arranged external grammar can be mentally intelligible. There would then appear to be two-layered identities at play, an inner rational identity of agency and an external social identity such as gender.

The structural potential for meaning originates in a separate mental space before encountering the biologically formed facility for phonemes and sounds. In the preceding Chapter 2 on cognitive linguistics, it was argued that, indeed, the capacity to conceptualize and form meaning occupied a different mental space than the capacity for the production of sound and that these two spaces came together to produce meaningful sounds. As already mentioned in a sociolinguistic paradigm, Vygotsky (1986) maintains that these two areas of conceptual capacity and sound come together from the age of 2–3 years and, once joined together progress towards higher-order thinking.

We need to acknowledge then that social meaning enters the biological sound system mediated by a mind-based conceptual system. Meaning then develops into higher-order thinking once these key elements have been brought together.

Language as construing the world

A very important point to note in Hallidayan systemic functional linguistic (henceforth SFL) is that, as Bache (2010) points out, there is a great emphasis on language as 'construing' the world rather than just representing or describing it. This is because of the emphasis on speaker agency and intentionality in her/his use of language and its use in social context rather than language as a static phenomenon. So, language as socially conceptualized is at the behest of the user and his/her intentionality. Therefore, the user uses language to interpret his/her own vision and perception of the world. Consequently, the two separate mental spaces of prelinguistic conceptual potential and phonemes are, as mentioned above, only places of origin. Once language is being used according to SFL, identity rests with the user in how he or she construes the word through language. This is an important shift in identity from previous chapters where identity was very much with the language and use was hardly considered if at all. Now the onus is with the user and his/her own agency to shape the world through language. And this is where the narrative of language moves towards user and user interpretation.

Grammatics – the theory of grammar

Bavali and Sadighi (2008) point out that grammar emerges in SFL (Systemic Functional Linguistics) from meaning and the creativity of making meaning. Grammar in SFL is an enabling device rather than a structural constraining device. Bavali and Sadighi argue that in SFL, 'language is a resource for making meanings and hence grammar is a resource for creating meaning by means of wording' (2008; p14). So unlike Chomskyan grammar, which is devoid of meaning, SFL grammar generates meaning as well as expressing pre-existing meaning, and is therefore more than a mechanical device.

Grammar in SFL is 'systemic'. It is the part of a system which allows for systemic choice. As Halliday says 'grammar's function is to construe; the grammar transforms experience into meaning, imposing order in the form of categories and their interrelations' (2002; p390). Therefore, grammar is a choice in how to orientate language in the framing of experience. For example, in a sentence does one choose an active voice with a subject pronoun to highlight agency or a passive voice so that the object of the sentence becomes the subject, in order to conceal agency. This is a choice that might need to be made in interpreting and linguistically framing experience and this choice may conceal a moral or ideological position. Consider the following language/grammar choices:

1 Five thousand redundancies had to be made at X.co.
2 X.co. made five thousand workers redundant.

A lexicogrammatical choice in example number one underplays agency in not highlighting who exactly is making the redundancies whereas example number two clearly states who is responsible for these redundancies. In choosing the first sentence, the writer might want to play down the responsibility for the redundancies.

Consequently, grammar in the SFL model is a system of choices and interpretations where the speaker or user chooses the grammatical devices to express his/her meaning from all the lexicogrammatical possibilities. Similar choices could be made in terms of other grammatical items such as verb tense. For example, when one wants to interpret an action in terms of a time frame. Another choice in interpretation could be one of subject pronoun where agency could again be hidden by using the impersonal 'one', thereby manufacturing a sense of authority by objectifying the action. 'One could argue that this is the case' has the authority of seeming objective as opposed to saying, 'I argue that this is the case'. Using 'one' instead of 'you' also avoids directly positioning someone and again manufactures objectivity. 'One does this' seems more objective than 'you do this'.

As well as 'systemic', SFL is functional in that it serves a purpose in its transmission of meaning. A key function of grammar is to abstract the individual from his/her present circumstances and project the mind of the individual into the future or back in the past. If we cast our minds back to the Linear Grammar of Cognitive Linguistics which is a skeleton of basic grammar following a basic causality of subject, action and object of action, we can see that such a primitive grammar is mentally restrictive. If this were all the grammar that ever existed, it would limit mental capacity to the present. One of the functions of grammar is to allow for projection into the future and, also to express memories of the past. Grammar allows for past experience to be converted into meaning. It is also relational in allowing a 'I' or 'We'–'You' relations or any combination of subject pronouns. For these and other reasons, grammar is functional. It serves functions of time and relations drawn from the materiality of experience.

In abstracting the individual from immediate experience in the present in the construction of past and future meanings, the meanings themselves become multilayered through grammatical devices such as relative adjectives and pronouns. The meanings come to refer to other words and meanings rather than directly to objects. Complex sentences using recursive grammatical devices such as relative adjectives and pronouns abstract the language user from direct experience in the present and liberate him/her from the restriction of lived local experience. So, a longer sentence can refer back to its constituent elements within the lexis rather than directly to the external world. Such grammatical functions make for the development of higher-order abstract thinking which a linear grammar without recursive devices would not be able to do. This includes detailed and complex descriptions which a writer such as the French writer, Marcel Proust, can undertake in his very long sentences enabled by relative clauses in which I have underlined the relative pronouns and adjectives as follows,:- 'The explanation for Mme de Cambremer's presence on this occasion was that the Princesse de Parme, devoid of snobbishness as are most truly royal personages, and by contrast eaten up with a pride in and passion for charity <u>which</u> rivalled her taste for <u>what</u> she believed to be the Arts, had bestowed a few boxes here and there upon women like Mme de Cambremer <u>who</u> were not numbered among the highest aristocratic society but with <u>whom</u> she was in communication with regard to charitable undertakings' (Marcel Proust – Guermantes' Way translated by C.K.S. Montcrieff and T. Kilmartin p51 1981 Chatto &Windus).

Proust is well known for his extraordinarily long sentences; however, without the relative adjectives and pronouns underlined such a long narration would have had to have been split up into several shorter sentences.

Without such complex grammar there would be no storytelling, there would be no referring back to lexis already mentioned within the sentence and separate simpler sentences would have to be used and there would be no flights of imagination into the future. Consequently, in terms of individual identity, grammatical function is necessary to liberate the individual from a restricted present and presence in language.

Lexicogrammar and identity

The use of grammar can construe or express the identity of the individual. Subject pronouns or naming devices as grammar are located at the root of identity formation. An immediate example of this is whether in speaking or writing we use the header 'I', 'We' or 'One'. Often a choice is being made as to whether we wish the verb to be centred on 'Me', in which case 'I' is used or collectively centred on 'Us' in which case 'We' is used. In other words, do we see ourselves as the lone individual in terms of identity or do we conceive of ourselves collectively as part of a group? Of course, this depends upon the social context and our identities can change from situation to situation. It might be neither of these identities that is chosen but rather the objective identity of the impersonal 'One'. The advantage of this latter pronoun is that it renders the ensuing verbal phrase as appearing to be objective and therefore personally disinterested, perhaps with a more authoritative claim for a truth proposition. Consequently, the grammar of subject pronouns allows us to personalize the identity of the action or render it impersonal. Returning to the appellation of 'Systemic Functional Linguistics', such grammatical choices and interpretations are afforded by the system in SFL and help to shape identity or situational subjectivity in immediate social context.

Social categories of gender are also reflected and constructed in grammar such as the subject pronouns of 'He', 'She' and neutral 'It' for objects as well as the Object Pronouns of 'His' and 'Hers' and the adjectives 'His' and 'Her'. A current debate occurs in the personal and social category of transgender concerning individuals in terms of the use of 'He' and 'She'. However, these two subject pronouns may very well not express the currently lived identity experience of those in transition and in this case, there may well be a debate to be had as to which subject pronouns could be used and even if there should be a new one.

Chevalier and Planté (2016) argue that, in the French language in particular, there is an explicit gender hierarchy in subject pronouns in the plural where 'they' or 'ils' is designated because the latter includes the feminine 'elles' in mixed gender company. So, when 'they' refers to all females, the feminine 'elles' is used as one would expect and when the company is all male, 'ils' is used for 'they' as one would expect but when it is mixed company, the masculine plural 'ils' takes precedence. Chevalier and Planté maintain that this gender hierarchy exposes 'the weight of grammatical system that imposes an omnipresent, restrictive, asymmetrical classification onto living beings and onto our perception of the world' (2016; p11.) Arguing from a French language perspective they maintain that gender ideology is contained within the language, not only due to subject pronouns but also continuing into adjectival endings in agreement with these gender-based subject pronouns. So we have the following example: –Les filles et les garçons sont part_is_ pour le centre-ville a neuf heures mais _ils_ n'étaient pas en retard pour le rendez-vous. (trans.: The girls and boys left for the town centre at nine o'clock, but they were not late for the meeting.) The lexicogrammatical items underlined take the masculine form even though the sentence refers to mixed gender company and this includes the past participle ending 'partis' taking the masculine form. However, the gender precedence applies also in adjectival agreements. So, we could have 'Les filles et les garçons ici présents sont très intelligents' where the two adjectives 'présents' and 'intelligents' are in the masculine plural form even though girls are present (trans.: the girls and boys present are very intelligent).

This gender bias in subject pronouns is less noticeable in Italian and Spanish which tend to drop the subject pronouns anyway in front of a verb. Spanish does not have past participle agreements with the verb in the past perfect tense although it does have gender- and number-based adjectival agreements.

Chevalier and Planté state that gender in language is a significant factor in cultural identity although they point out that it is not clear whether language helps to construct gender or whether it simply marks and reinforces gender. It is nevertheless true that in English as well as French and other languages, the 'He', 'She' dichotomy forces a choice between male and female since grammatically, at the moment of writing in 2021, there is no transgender subject pronoun category in widespread mainstream conventional use, outside of any transgender community.

Nominalization

Hart (2014) proposes that ' no linguistic structure is in and of itself ideological – at least not in the pejorative sense' (2014; p36). The forgoing gender-orientated constructions in the last section would not substantiate this claim, given the precedence of the masculine over the feminine in mixed gender settings.

However, Hart does point out that grammatical nominalization can be used to categorize individuals negatively or in a way in which they appear excluded and 'not one of us'. In this sense nominalization is the way of naming through the use of an adjective or a verb as a noun.

Let us consider the following imagined examples from football match media commentary where nationality is mentioned as follows: 'Olivier Giroud has scored yet again for Chelsea. That makes the 29th goal scored for Chelsea by the Frenchman' (my example). This sort of commentary occurs many times concerning non-British players when nationality nominalizations are used in match commentaries. Other examples could be 'The Dutchman', 'The Uruguayan' or 'The Brazilian', etc. An actual example is as follows in an English Premier League match between Wolves (Wolverhampton Wanderers) and Newcastle United in a BBC TV Match of the Day Commentary on Saturday 2 October 2021: Commenting on a goal just scored by Wolves, the commentator remarked, 'it's a delightful finish for the South Korean'. This referred to the Wolves forward Hwang Hee-Chan. However, in a league football match the commentator would never say the 'The Englishman' in his/her commentary because it would be expected as normative given that the Premier League is English and yet there are very few English players in the top teams in this league.

The possible effect of this is that the nominalization of 'English' is not mentioned because it is normative, even though in the top teams there are fewer English players than those of other nationalities. The nominalization of other nationalities however is mentioned and serves to be exclusive as 'not one of us' but of another category.

Hart quotes an explicit example of such exclusion as follows: 'If he is to live as a British citizen, then he must have the ability to integrate into the society of his chosen home. The immigrant owes that to himself as well as to his host society' (Norman Tebbit in the Independent newspaper 4 September 2003) (Hart 2014; p34). In this quotation we can see a double discrimination firstly one of gender in referring to the immigrant as 'he' and secondly as in excluded in the nominalization 'the immigrant'. So, the 'immigrant' is negatively objectified as not being one of us and not belonging to the 'host' society.

Subject pronouns can be used in an inclusion/exclusion dichotomy especially in the use of 'We' and when used by an individual in interaction as a substitution for 'I' to aggrandize power as well as to underline his/her community belonging. We can see this in the imagined dialogue between an employer and a potential employee at interview. (My example)

> Employer: 'We would take you on as a part-time contract in the first instance'
> Employee: 'How long would this contract last?'

Here the hiring manager is using an inclusive 'We' to include him into a belonging to management, but this is also exclusive in the exercise of power which the potential employee does not possess, thereby emphasizing the power differential between the two individuals.

Therefore, the grammar of subject pronouns, naming and nominalization has an impact on identity in highlighting who has the power and the inclusion/exclusion of who is 'in' and who is 'out'.

Verbs, ideology and identity

Verb tenses and moods allow us to expand our identity across time and also to conceal our identity. In this way we can make an authoritative impersonal statement by saying 'It is thought that ....', making the statement appear to be objective or if we say, 'It is expected that ....' An impersonal authoritative command.

More positively, we can project identity into the future by expressing 'What I will do' and 'what I will be' as well as recalling the past. We can also use a continuous tense in the present to emphasize something that is 'being done' which in SFL is a grammatical choice to be made if confronted with a question such as 'Why has this not been done?' The pressure of such a question leaves the present continuous as a grammatical option where one might not be able to say that something 'will be done' because that is too far in the future. Instead that something 'is being done' might give the appropriate immediacy of the present when clearly something is not already done.

More subtly we have a grammatical option to express doubt and uncertainty in the use of the subjunctive mood and this can soften an ideological position. For example, 'If this is the case, then … … ' can soften to 'If this be the case, then ….'; using the subjunctive 'be' rather than the indicative 'is'. The subjunctive mood here expresses doubt about the existence of 'the case'.

The subjunctive mood and identity

The world of the subjunctive is not a definite world of fixed and firm identity but an equivocal one of 'maybe' and 'perhaps'. Such and such could happen if this were to be the case, but this is not really likely. Consequently, the grammar of the subjunctive is not solid or permanent and the user of this mood is in a position of equivocating. The user of the indicative might say of a situation, 'It is what it is' – a phrase that we hear often now in the media. The use of the subjunctive alternatively would equivocate his/her identity within the context of the situation by saying something like, 'Be that as it may'. The latter phrase in the subjunctive is not being definitive about the present state of affairs, saying it could be the case rather than it is the case. The subjunctive expresses images and metaphors and offers up an alternative to the indicative world of fact. If we were only ever able to use the factual language of the indicative, the conceptualization of wishing for something better might never occur and identity would be much more matter of fact and less wishful and idealistic since we could no longer say, 'If only this were the case ….'. The subjunctive mood is therefore an identity of imagination and the potential for creatively imagining that such and such could be the case even though patently it is not.

In referring to Isaac Newton, Romanyshyn (2015) argues that 'And we have taken up his (Newton's) – (my parenthesis) way of languaging the world, the language of science whose indicative mood has severed fact from fantasy, reason from dream, mind from soul and has privileged the former over the latter' (2015; p7).

Conclusion

In this chapter we have seen the externally facing social aspects of grammar in interaction with the social context of language. We have seen how grammar in its social context is part of the general nature of lexis as lexicogrammar, using words from the lexicon but corresponding to internal conceptualizations of grammar such as agency, time, causality and uncertainty of causality. Grammar here seems to be rationally produced although socially shaped. Of course, within this progression in grammar towards an external social nature, we move from formal linguistics to applied linguistics and we move across paradigm boundaries that Halliday himself did not recognize as intrinsically valid or indeed helpful in understanding that both the nature and function of language are inextricably linked. We see this relationship between language and its function in the next chapter, Chapter 4, in Saussure's notion of 'Langue' and 'Parole', referring in the former to the structural nature of language and in the latter to how language is used socially. A caveat must be inserted here that Halliday insists that grammar has meaning and is more than a rational device for intelligibility. Therefore, for SFL, grammar does join up the nature of language to its use in viewing grammar on a continuum with lexis and indeed, at least at surface level, as arising out of lexis.

The chapter discussed how SFL regards meaning as social and generated within the social interaction of language users. This means that users shape language for their own intentions through their acts of meaning-making. Consequently, language becomes a means of constructing as well as describing the world.

To conclude, the SFL model of language is such that it is shaped by the user to achieve certain functional outcomes and we have had examples of these functions in language users' ability to express choices and interpretations for meaning within language as 'systemic'.

In the next chapter, we will focus on semantics, in how words take on different meanings in different social contexts across time and place and in doing so become saturated with the intentions, identity subject positions and again the interpretations of language users.

4

Structuralism

In this chapter I argue that the basis for interpretation in language and subsequent identity is the break between the signifier and the signified. So, if the signifier is the word – sound, and the signified is the object – concept, these two are not the same thing. The word is not the object, they have been joined together by conventional agreement but in essence there is a gap between them. Consequently, in essence they are not the same thing and for this reason, the word – sound and the object – idea which both, in joining together, constitute the sign, need interpretation. The sign therefore does not represent any notion of an underlying reality; it is simply associated with an idea of reality. The consequences for identity might be viewed as somewhat disconcerting where identity is no longer grounded in a word-object lexis as in Wittgenstein's Tractatus and in the rationality of Sameness but rather in interpretation as Difference, where a word can have different meanings. A word as a phoneme sound is indeed a hollow shell before any number of meanings is attached as a result of sociocultural association. Often a word only comes to its intended meaning in the context of the utterance by the speaker and if taken out of context, the meaning can be misconstrued. An example of this is where a word at the same time could have both a literal and a metaphorical meaning such as 'Light'. If someone states out of context that s/he has seen the light, the meaning could be physical, that the person has indeed seen the morning dawn break in light or the person has suddenly understood a deeper reality.

Furthermore, due to the signifier–signified disconnection, word meanings can change, rendering meanings interpretable and therefore fluid; this has an impact of identity. It means that identity no longer has a sure footing in a restricted semantic space but becomes open to the world and exploratory in terms of different cultures or ideologies. Perhaps disconcerting to some but exciting and liberating to others.

Introduction to Ferdinand de Saussure's structuralism

Sounds as phonemes of course are empty noises, as would be the sound of an unfamiliar or foreign word that needs a meaning to be attached for the learner of a new language. So how does a sound or phoneme come to mean something and then perhaps over time change its meaning into something else?

Ferdinand de Saussure has been described as the father of modern linguistics and it is to his seminal work, *The Course of General Linguistics* (1916) that we must refer in order to answer these questions.

The journey of this book is a progression towards language as interpretation, because language eventually becomes, as Saussure (1916) points out many times, a social institution and at one and the same time, both mental and social. For Chomsky, the mental comes first whereas for Saussure, language is an agreed social convention before becoming subsequently lodged in the minds of individuals. It does not repose on a solid ground of reality and its constituent words are arbitrary in that a word-sound can mean what the current convention wants it to mean.

This chapter which draws heavily on Ferdinand de Saussure goes beyond grammar as an autonomous entity and views the whole of language as a social system where all semantic items depend on each other. In explicating language, Saussure states that '…it is a system of signs in which the only essential thing is the union of meanings and sound-images' (1916; p15). So, for Saussure it is a semantic system as opposed to a Chomskyan grammatical system. A word is not an object but comes, by agreement, to designate an object-idea by association. Saussure does not go back to the very origins of language to conjecture upon how the very first word-sounds came into being and so, meaning in its historical beginnings still remains a mystery in terms of how the first sounds and objects were originally united into a sign. However, he does in his study of synchronic linguistics explain how sound-word and object unite in the context of the sound-meaning social environment where signs are already in current usage; human beings having already been born into an existing language system.

So, Saussure states that 'the linguistic sign unites not a thing and a name but a concept and a sound-image. The concept and the sound then exist in "close association seemingly as one" and "prompt each other"' (1916; p66).

Therefore, there is nothing in a word-sign such as 'house' that inherently means a large dwelling of four walls or 'car' as a metal bodywork on four wheels propelled by an engine. The word-signs 'car' and 'house' are entirely arbitrary and could have designated entirely different objects, if over time they had been in association with these different objects.

Saussure explains that the word-sign is like a two-way plug into which, on one side of the sign a physical sound is plugged in, and, on the other side, an idea or object is plugged in. So, the sound is the signifier, and the object-idea is the signified and both together, these two constitute the sign. Without this two-way plug, the sound is just a noise without meaning and the idea-object is a shapeless mass or vague feeling. This is highlighted upon hearing a foreign language of which one has no knowledge, which is a meaningless and continuous linear sound. The sound needs to be differentiated into units which read across to specific items of reality. So, both sides need differentiation which is a bracketing of both sound on one side of the equation and idea-object, on the other side, in parallel, so that they can come together as united by social convention. It is in this regard that Saussure regards language as a system of differences.

Mediaeval language of sameness

In 'The Order of Things', Michel Foucault looks back historically at language and identity in the pre-scientific era before the Enlightenment and tells of how language was conceived as natural sign along with the natural world of plants, stars and planets. In this pre-scientific era, the word and the thing were one, as the word revealed the object as a sign left by the divine for man/woman to discover. Foucault explains as follows: 'In the original form, when it was given to men by God himself, language was an absolutely certain and transparent sign for things, because it resembled them. The names of things were lodged in the things they designated … … … ' (2002; p40).

Therefore, according to Foucault, not only was it thought that natural signs such as movement of planets in the cosmos were the imprint of the divine in the universe but language itself was a divine attribute. Foucault refers to the Port Royal grammarians as asserting that the signified and the signifier were inherently connected so that the word was the thing. Language was then a natural sign as Foucault explicates this historical view, 'Language partakes in the worldwide dissemination of similitudes and signatures. It must therefore be studied itself as a thing in nature' (2002; p39).

Foucault is highlighting a very religious world view where all knowledge was esoteric and divinely imprinted on the earth for our discovery as an expression of God's revelation. So before human construction of the sciences such as chemistry, there was already alchemy, before biology as a science there were natural signs, before astronomy, stargazing was about astrology. Language in the same way was only important as written language which was, for the most part, expressed in holy texts for mystical deciphering. So, Foucault explains that in this era, 'Divination is not a rival form of knowledge; it is part of the main body of knowledge' (2002; p36). Since the Enlightenment, in the modern era and the age of science, natural phenomena are the subject of analysis and explanation as opposed to divination. The realization that the signified is disconnected from the signifier means that words and language depend on each other for meaning as a system and are not part of any divine revelation per se in an ordinary sense. Since the Enlightenment, science has widened and generated many subdivisions and new sciences have emerged, social sciences as subdivisions of philosophy, such as psychology, sociology and linguistics. These subjects relate to each other in that the constituent elements of these subjects under consideration relate to each other laterally as opposed to vertically and upwards to the divine, as would have been the case prior to the scientific age of the Enlightenment. Consequently, there is a lateral dispersal where new language and discourses have evolved and proliferated, and especially with the rise of audiovisual media and now social networks. Language is then used in different ways such as the notion of 'trending' in social media such as 'Twitter'. In former times no one would have announced that a particular theme or subject was 'trending' signposted by a 'hashtag'. Indeed, many people who are not conversant with social media may still have no understanding at all of this new language to express that a particular subject has prominence in discussion. Therefore, with new subjects, new media language has broadened out and words are used in different ways as part of different discourses now far removed from the mediaeval view of one word – one meaning in the hierarchical connection between the divine and man/woman.

This disconnection of the signified from the signifier is a deconstruction of the sign as linguistics also established itself as a science by Ferdinand de Saussure. Unless language is one's focus of study and analysis, it is difficult for many people to imagine a word hollowed out of its conventional meaning and reduced to a phoneme which theoretically could then, by association, be ready to mean something different. For many people, especially English-speaking monolinguals, a structure with four walls and a roof can be no other than the English word 'house' and one cannot imagine the word 'house' meaning anything else. In practice then the word and the thing are still one and the same, but this is by association and not divinely ordained to be so. The argument for language education is to widen this perspective to show that a word can indeed take on many meanings.

Saussure's disconnection of the signified from the signifier does relativize language, differentiate meanings and consequently identities, dispersing language out horizontally or laterally for multiple interpretations away from the simple identity of one word, one intrinsic meaning.

Language as difference

Saussure states that 'Language has neither ideas nor sounds that existed before the linguistic system **and** it is only conceptual and phonic differences that have issued from the linguistic system' (Ferdinand de Saussure 1916; p120). Further on he states, 'A linguistic system is a series of differences of sound combined with a series of differences of ideas' (1916; p120). The second quote does seem to contradict the first one because in the second quote he mentions reference to ideas whereas in the first quote he states that ideas do not exist independently of language and indeed have no existence prior to the linguistic system. Although ideas are not defined before language, Saussure does seem to suggest that there is a pairing or matching between sound and a chain of perceptions or ill-defined thoughts. I find that the Course in General Linguistics is unclear as to what language as a continuous chain of sound is supposed to be mapped against if it is not some kind of vague mass of thought-feeling.

However, this means that the meaning that occurs between the sound-word of the signifier and the object-idea of the signified depends upon difference on both sides of the matching divide. In order for meaning to occur both sides need to be delimited so that the continuous sound chain that one hears in language learning needs to be broken down into units of meaning. This means that the continuous mass of incoherent reality also needs to be delineated against the continuous chain of sound. Meaning is then based upon delineation and difference so that one thing means something because it does not mean another thing. If, for example, one is learning what the sound-word 'tree' means, it has to be differentiated from the objects around it so that it does not end up meaning something else such as a 'bush'. So, a tree is a tree because it is differentiated with 'not a tree'. Different languages dissect reality in different ways and so there may be a language-culture which does not make the same 'decoupage' or differentiation that for example English- or French language-culture makes.

We will look at differences in meanings across English and French for what are the same words and how they are sometimes framed differently in a later section of this chapter.

A grammatical example of such differentiation is in subject pronouns because we know that 'I' relates to 'me', as opposed to other persons such as 'You' and vice versa, in that 'You' differentiates from 'I'. Someone who does not want to make such a differentiation might use the impersonal 'One' in the verbal phrase but here again the act of doing this is also one of differentiation in wanting to avoid personalization of an action. 'I' also differentiates from 'We' and overuse of 'I' may give the impression of individualism and refusal to view oneself as an integral part of community. This is because when one says 'I', in order for 'I' to have meaning it has to exclude anything which is 'not I'. So 'I' means 'not you' and 'not we'. Such subject pronoun differentiation reflects an individual awareness of separation from others and yet at the same time there is a grammatical association with other subject pronouns simply because subject pronouns are grammatically related, just as people are humanly related and connected. 'I' is differentiated from 'You' and yet at the same time to express 'I' acknowledges that there is a 'not I' which connects us to the other 'not I's' of 'You', 'She/He', 'They', etc. Subject pronouns might be different from each other but nonetheless they are all subjects and consequently, grammatically related as agents of actions. In the same way with objects there is similarity, in for example, the word for 'trees' where all examples of the 'tree' category resemble each other yet are distinct from the category of 'bushes'. Therefore objects, through similarity, are within the same generic category whilst at the same time the generic category can only exist in binary opposition to other categories. Furthermore, there is a myriad of differences with regard to the different types of trees, so, we begin a process of differentiation where an oak tree is an oak because it resembles other oaks but differentiates itself from that which is 'not oak' in a binary opposition. This can go on and on if there are different types of oak trees. However, this is an example of this book's definition of identity which emerges out of a relationship between Sameness and Difference expressed within language.

There is a sense that something does not exist fully until it is evoked and delineated in language and if one fails to acknowledge the word and therefore meaning, one then suppresses identity. We will see later that the binary where 'A' exists because it is not 'not A' means a suppression of reality and culture for that which has not been highlighted to have a meaning. Now this is relevant in certain binaries such as 'man', 'woman' where often 'man' is used as a universal human category and 'not man' (woman as a suppressed category) disappears from view. We will see in Chapter 8 that Derrida's concept of deconstruction is a process of unpicking such binaries to reveal other possible meanings which have been suppressed. In this way the 'not something' always has a trace to existence through its absence. An analogy of this would be a person who is conspicuous through their absence.

Therefore, language and meaning rely on difference but also on similarity so that we can categorize the world. Human identity equally rests on both sameness and difference through language. We acknowledge ourselves as human through the constituent parts expressed in language that unite us physically, mentally and often spiritually as human so that we share in a common humanity. However, at the same time, within common humanity, we express difference, linguistically constructing through language our different cultures. When languages in the world are suppressed such as the language of Uyghurs in north-west China (Evans 2015; Evans 2018) then, as a consequence, cultural identity comes under threat and has to struggle to survive for its continued existence.

Time

Time plays a vital role in the association between sound and idea in the formation of the sign. Given that the sign is psychological and consequently does not relate directly to the outside world, why are signs relatively stable? If sound-concept associations change, why is it that word sign meanings do not change overnight or week by week?

Saussure explains this by stating that word meanings are held in place by the other word meanings in the sentence because words in a sentence are interdependent – they do not stand in isolation. So, word meanings are held in place, internally, by other word meanings in the sentence and externally by social convention. The notion of social convention shaping word meanings is an early foretaste of the role of power. However, Saussure's linguistics is devoid of references to external ideological pressure beyond the neutral label of conventional agreement. He does not deconstruct or unpack social agreement in terms of who holds the power to decide upon meanings and, in the Course of General Linguistics there is no mention of the authority of dictionaries in shaping semantics. We will come to this in the next chapter (Chapter 5) with a focus on sociolinguistics and discourse where power is introduced in the construction of meaning. In terms of Saussurean structural linguistics, Saussure declares that the signifier is 'bound to the existing language' (1916; p71). Continuity is then a stabilizing force.

Conversely, time itself can act as an enabling force where, over much longer periods, meanings evolve culturally. So, time is a force by virtue of the space it allows for linguistic development, and over time meaning slippage can occur between word-sound signifier and object-idea signified. Some words have a physical meaning and then, over time whilst still retaining their original meaning, develop another meaning at a different cultural level. The verb 'to modernize' has its obvious meaning of bringing up to date. However, in another foretaste of the power behind ideological meanings, this verb has also come to mean modernizing with regard to workforce practices and often this means efficiencies in working conditions where examples could mean extending working hours, reducing breaks, assuming extra skills, performance indicators and responsibilities through further training. In this regard the concept of 'to modernize' is often no longer neutral but ideological.

Another very common example where meaning has changed is frequently quoted in the use of the adjective 'Gay' where in Victorian English, it meant merry or jolly. This adjectival meaning is no longer used, and the adjective has evolved or rather been developed by users to mean 'Homosexual'. The adjective has now entered the French language and its entry in 'Le Robert' dictionary is 'gay- adjectif et nom- Homosexuel'. However, the French word 'Gai' (masculine), 'Gaie' (feminine) spelt in the traditional French way is still retained to mean merry or joyous which is no longer the case in English.

Therefore, language and meaning are subject to both the social forces of continuity and, also change over time.

Changes over time within language: Langue and parole

Because there is no intrinsic value in a word sign and notwithstanding the constraints of social convention, there is no inherent reason, as we have seen, why over time a word has to be tied to the same object.

Furthermore, Saussure separates language into 'Langue' and 'Parole' which align respectively with linguistic notions of 'Competence' and 'Performance'.

The competence side of language or 'Langue' is the totality of the linguistic system. Saussure states that 'Language is a store-house filled by members of a given community through the active use of speaking' (1916; p13). Further on he states, 'In separating language from speaking, we are separating what is social language from what is individual speech.' Speech is then a personalized function of the systemic convention of language and so Parole is then the practice of spoken language in social context. Parole is akin to a personalized twist on the system, but which nonetheless relies on the system for its underlying meaning. So, it draws upon the system since functions of individualized speech which did not draw upon an agreed conventional semantic system would make no sense. 'Langue' is agreed by the community and is held in place by communal agreement of what words mean. Langue and Parole are interdependent in that the latter as speech draws upon the more formal Langue for its meaning, generating variations in meanings in interactions with everyday life in sociocultural context. Over time the informal meanings in Parole feed back into Langue as language develops. This means that the spoken language of everyday life in different cultural contexts gives rise to semantic slippages between words and objects-ideas. These are not huge differences in meaning but rather slight modifications of meaning which often can be seen to be connected to the more formally agreed meaning of Langue. This is not to say that, theoretically, and over time, meanings cannot develop/evolve more radically so that they do not appear to bear much relation to their original formal meaning. Furthermore, the more culturally localized meanings of Parole can also become empowered conventionally to such an extent that they re-enter Langue as conventionally agreed meanings. Therefore, Parole can feed back into Langue and so the two are closely interrelated. Conversely, many changes in meaning within Parole never become conventionalized and never re-enter the standard.

An example of adjectives drawn from the standard language of Langue which develop different meanings but never re-enter conventional language are often examples taken from youth language in adjectives such as 'sick', 'insane' and the more dated 'wicked'. In conventional terms such adjectives are negative implying illness or malice but in youth language they have been turned on their head to mean excellent. They can be connected back to their formal origins in Langue because they are opposite of their original meaning. Another youth-generated adjective which has changed its meaning from a physical quality to a moral/aesthetic note of approval is 'cool'. The conventional adjective denotes 'freshness' and we can see how it has been used by a youth culture, first of all to denote 'laid back', meaning that one did not get worked up and 'hot under the collar' about situations and so one remained 'cool'. The journey of the adjective has moved on to 'cool' meaning 'trendy' or 'far out' (away from convention) and finally many young people use 'cool' to simply mean 'yes' or 'agreed'. So, there is slippage of meaning from the original sign, but the meaning trajectory appears to be logically connected to its original meaning. One day 'cool' might become a dictionary alternative to 'yes'.

In France, in the housing estates around Paris there is an urban dialect called Verlan which is a back slang where words and word syllables are pronounced backwards so that for example the word for 'woman' in conventional language 'femme' becomes 'meuf'. Other examples are 'un bus' becomes 'un sub', 'une soeur' – sister becomes 'une reus', 'un père' – father becomes 'un reup' and with words of more than one syllable, the syllables are reversed as follows: – 'bizarre' becomes 'zarbi', 'pourri' – rotten becomes 'ripou' and 'louche' – shady becomes 'chelou'. Again, the slang meaning is related to the original in the reverse spelling. In the UK, there is a similar urban dialect in the East End of London known as Cockney Rhyming Slang where spelling is the unique connection to the original in its rhyme. Examples of this are 'apples and pears' – 'stairs', 'whistle and flute' – suit, 'trouble and strife' – wife, 'butcher's hook' – look. Two things to be noted here are that the dialect seems gendered in the last but one of the expressions unless there is the equivalent to denote and rhyme with 'husband' and secondly the last expression is now more generalized as slang in other parts of the country where people will talk about 'having a butcher's' at something meaning 'to have a look'. Again, it should be noted that language use in informal contexts such as urban dialects expresses and generates identity characteristics of Sameness and Difference. Sameness because urban dialects such as Verlan in Paris and Cockney Rhyming slang in London both bind users together and at the same time exclude and differentiate against non-users. In some cases, this may be intended as a rebellion against Establishment power as in Verlan on the housing estates of France.

Over much longer periods of time there are changes in standard conventional language or 'Langue' where words have changed their meaning more gradually. We can see this is Biblical language in King James Bible of 1611 translated into English from Greek and Hebrew. Examples of words whose original meanings are different from current usage are 'Meat' and 'Letters'. In the Gospel of John, Jesus says, 'Labour not from the meat which perisheth but for the meat which endureth into everlasting life … … ' (John, chapter 6; verse 27). The meaning of 'meat' here is food generally as opposed to animal flesh, which is the modern-day usage of 'meat'.

The word 'letters' was formerly 'knowledge' as opposed to the alphabet or mail. In the Gospel of John in referring to Jesus we find the quote, 'How knoweth this man letters, having never learned?' (John, chapter 6; verse 15). Of course, this historical meaning is still evidenced in the expressions 'a man' or 'woman' of letters but in current usage no longer means knowledge.

Much more recently in standard language the historical meanings of words such as 'Spinster' and 'Bachelor' have changed. Indeed, the word 'Spinster' for an unmarried woman is now hardly ever used. However, its origin is a woman who worked alone spinning yarn on a spinning wheel. The idea of solitude evolved from a mode of work into a mode of life. A 'Bachelor' similarly means an unmarried man but historically denoted a mediaeval knight. Presumably one could conjecture that the etymology of bachelor related to being young and unmarried as a feature of knighthood.

Semantic changes within cultures and discourses

Many words change from standard meanings to developing more specific meanings within a professional cultural discourse. Legal settings have examples of words which are standard in conventional language but assume a different flavour when used in a legal setting. Here are a few examples: bar, chamber, silk, bench, dock, and the way their meanings have changed albeit still traceable to the standard meaning as follows:

The Bar- the profession of barrister

Chamber- a judge's room whereas in old English it designated a bedroom

Silk- a Queen's Council barrister

Bench- a judge's seat.

Dock- the defendant's seat

Crown- the prosecution, as it is the monarch who prosecutes because the law belongs to the King or Queen and not to the people.

Word meanings change then within separate cultural discourses, and they also change as they move from one language to another, as we see in the next section.

Semantic changes across languages

Word meanings are shaped then by the culture in which they are used and as such we can see the same words in the following examples in French whose meanings are modified when they are imported into English. These are not complete changes but often slight modifications which emphasize a slightly different alternative meaning when used in English, not forgetting that in both languages a word can carry several dictionary meanings. Some examples are as follows:

> 'A cortege' in English is specifically a funeral procession whereas in the original French meaning it can be any sort of procession.

> 'A dossier' in English is a completed file or a file being completed whereas in French it can be a physical object that you buy from a stationer.

> 'A doyen/doyenne' in English denotes a person, male or female who is senior in terms of culture or knowledge whereas in French it can mean someone senior simply in terms of age, as well as knowledge/culture (in old French un/e doyen/nne was the head of a university).

> 'Le dressage' in English relates to equestrian skills whereas in French it is the training of any animal.

> 'Une escapade' in English means a reckless adventure whereas in French it means an escape in the sense of a tourist destination i.e., a luxury escape to an exotic holiday resort.

> 'Une liaison' in English is a close personal or relational connection with someone whereas in French it can also be a travel connection.

> 'Un canard' in English is a groundless story or rumour whereas in French it is a duck or in slang a sugar cube soaked in liqueur, a false musical note, as well as a groundless story.

Often these words imported from the French have a specific meaning in English where one meaning strand has been imported from the French rather than the whole meaning.

Sometimes the meaning changes in a different grammatical context in the example of the English word imported from the French 'Touché' meaning acknowledgement of the emotional impact of someone's comment. This is never used as an interjection in French, outside of a 'hit' in sword fencing, but instead used in a sentence such as 'j'étais touché par sa gentillesse' – 'I was touched by her/his kindness'.

Such meaning changes do not occur overnight but over time, varying from shorter periods of high interactivity such as youth language or longer periods of development in standard language as in the historical examples we have seen. Slippage of meaning takes time whether over a longer period in Langue or a shorter period in Parole because of the proximity in the gap between the signified and the signifier, 'in the case of Parole'. Such proximity is so close to the point that it may seem that the word is indeed the object rather than just designating it. This illusion of closeness in the association between the two is such that the signifier and the signified reciprocally evoke each other so that words can indeed construe and shape the world. The everyday experience is indeed that the utterance of a word elicits the object in such a way as to bring it into view. When ideology enters into this construal of the world, ideological constructions can become normalized and accepted as the natural order of things; and where the only way to unpick this, in order to see a wider range of possible meanings, is through a process of deconstruction. We will encounter deconstruction in the chapter on poststructuralism in Part Four of this book.

Therefore, one should not forget Saussure's discovery in that it shatters the illusion that word and the object, although seemingly entering into each other through close association, are indeed not the same thing but rather separated as the signifier and signified, respectively.

The flaw in this system of meaning, which Saussure states arises from conventional community or societal agreement, is that it lacks a generative power of agency. If the generative power is not found within the nature of language as a system, then it must be from people as agents. When one talks about community meaning or societal meaning, one eventually must ask, 'Whose voice powers or generates the meaning?' There may be lots of meanings and yet some meanings prevail over others and if a word can attract many meanings one meaning may dominate and marginalize others. There is then a human factor inside this although Saussure makes it seem an objective system, especially since Saussure was only interested in language as a system and not at all in Parole as the way people speak in their social groups.

Presence

Roesler (2015) quotes the French poet Bonnefoy's critique of the Saussurean system as lacking presence. The presence of speakers resides in Parole and yet Saussure has no interest in the speaking subject. The users of Parole live their lives through language as it is spoken as opposed to a language system. Meanings are, as we have seen, more readily changed or modified in lived situations and the new modified meanings may not make their way back into Langue but instead remain as street, urban or rural language. Roesler argues that Bonnefoy's view of Parole is that it is much larger than the system of Langue in that it goes beyond the boundaries of the system to evoke speaker presence. Here the speaker inhabits the utterances he/she is making. Therefore, the language system itself is conceptual but not real life, whereas the spoken language is the embodiment of human presence.

For Saussure however, Parole is a fleeting presence, it is here and then gone in the speakers' utterance and not worthy of study. Saussure then remains interested only in the structure of language and not the enactment of it. The enactment of spoken language in terms of how it is used in social life within social groups had to wait for the development of sociolinguistics for its research and study. In the chapters and seminal linguists that we have looked at so far, neither Chomsky nor Saussure had any interest in this area of spoken language. By contrast, sociolinguistic research goes beyond decontextualized words and phrases and into the exploration and analysis of text as a whole, in terms of user discourse in social context. This expanding interest in social language which we will encounter in Part Three addressing sociolinguistics and discourse should not however negate the language and grammar of psychology, cognition and the mind. Both Langue as the language of the social mind and Parole as the language of social context are joined together conceptually in terms of a cognitive model of linguistics. Conceptually based linguistics refers us back to the Cognitive Linguistics of Chapter 3 and, in this regard, Holvoet (2020) argues that the language that reflects our conceptual structures imposes categories and borders on a continuous reality. For example, if there were not in terms of countries, geopolitical concepts of France and Spain, there would just be continuous terrain signifying nothing more than high altitudes and mountains. Consequently, in structural linguistics, although we have seen that words change in meaning over time and place, they change with reference to the developmental nature of culture.

Saussurean linguistics would suggest that it is language itself which shapes the culture as the culture does not pre-exist language independently. The sign itself categorizes and it does so by framing reality differently over different cultures. Holvoet (2020) refers to the speaker as an agent of conceptualization mediating between language and the non-linguistic world. It is the speaker then who is constructing conceptualization rather than just representing or describing reality as though it has its own independent existence. The speaker is the active user of language and responsible as such for language use in her/his choice of words and how they all join together in a discourse. We cannot just say that language has its identity in its categorizations of the world independently of the user of language. Identity then can be seen as divided between both language as a historical system in terms of 'Langue' and the way it is shaped into current discourse by the user in his/her groups which is 'Parole'. Discourse itself can be defined as a grouping together of concepts of similarity and although Saussure states, 'A language system is a series of differences of sound combined with a series of differences of idea', when seen, as a whole there are also associations of similarity between constructed ideas and, by extension the words which construct these ideas.

Sameness in discourse

Therefore, language as a whole arises not only out of differentiation between word and ideas but also associations between similar ideas and the words that designate them. To return to the earlier example of trees, although there are differences between trees so that an oak differs from a beech and from an ash and from a poplar etc. (all that is 'not oak'), these trees nonetheless, in spite of their named differences, form a commonality under the generic concept of tree displaying general similarities. Consequently, one can engage in a generic discourse of trees, especially if one works professionally in forestry where one deals with trees as a whole.

This applies to other areas such as education with associated concepts such as training, pedagogy, assessment, certification, students, classroom, learning, etc. One could cite other professional discourses such as the military, medicine, economic and finance, transport, football, etc., where all these areas form their own associations of meaning designated by language and the user's way of deploying language. Such discourses formed by language constructing similar associated ideas nevertheless, much in the same way as words, define their boundaries by excluding that which is 'not' the discourse in question. So, a football discourse preserves its identity as such because it is not another type of discourse, but we should not forget that discourses that seem set in stone have been constructed by their users. Football discourse is then constructed in its vocabulary and word structures by footballers, coaches, managers, commentators and fans, over many years.

Conclusion

We have seen in this chapter that language is not rooted in the natural order of the world, in that there is not a one-for-one reading between word and object. The gap between signifier and signified gives rise to a potential slippage of meaning.

Meanings are however held in place, grammatically by the functions of other words in the sentences internally and externally, in terms of word semantics by social convention. Grammatically a noun will still be a noun, even though often in English it can be turned into a verb such as 'to party' from the noun 'a party'. So, grammatical categories are stable; relative pronouns in English are often left out but such ellipsis leaves a gap for their insertion – such as in the example. 'The car I bought' which means 'The car that I bought' and the place is left open for the relative 'that' to be inserted. In French and Spanish for example, the relative has to be made explicit.

Meanings change and, as we have seen, are more likely to involve word semantics in interaction with sociocultural context, as this changes and develops. The corollary of all this is that grammatical structure is stable as the interior of language reflecting mental structures whereas word meanings are social, subject to change as they are the externally facing features of language.

The linguistic progression in this book argues that word meanings ultimately are shaped by social use and by extension social users of language in social groups. As Halliday (2003) argued, formal linguistics and sociolinguistics exploring language use are not mutually exclusive in a 'zero sum' game but rather ought to complement each other as they focus on different aspects of language and its use. With the progression of the book in the next section shifting from language towards language use, the focus of identity continues to move to the user and to the language in terms of a resource at the disposal of the user rather than as an objective system of Langue. The corollary of this is that users interpret language in the verbal and spoken texts that they deploy since their choice of words and construction of meaning arise from their interpretation of social context. Speakers are then speaking and using words from a particular position, using language to express and constitute their being in the world. This notion of being in the world expressed through words, groups of words extending out into text is known as discourse.

In the next chapter we will focus in more detail on what constitutes discourse and how discourses are shaped by speakers to reflect and construct identity in their sociocultural groups and contexts. We will also see how power generates meaning in discourse in terms of whose voice is heard and whose meanings prevail; and how highly powered discourses can cross over boundaries to colonize less powerful discourses.

Part Three

Interpretation

5

Sociolinguistics and Discourse

In this chapter we acknowledge, firstly, the understanding gained from Saussurean structuralism and secondly, we explore the implications of this understanding for sociolinguistics and discourse. In the notions of discourse, we move from the emphasis of identity being in the language to the emphasis of identity on the user where language becomes the user's resources for his/her social and cultural needs and objectives.

We have seen that language is not grounded in the natural order of the world and the development of language is cultural rather than natural. Vygotsky (1986) supports the view that language is developed culturally in a dialectical relationship with conceptual structures, which both combine together to develop higher-order thinking. Since the 'word' is a sociocultural sign, it is then disconnected the object. As we have seen, Saussure stated that the signified and the signifier were separated and only linked together by conventional association. He also stated that meanings could retain some stability due to the interdependence between lexical items in sentences. Consequently, we can see that language is social and therefore cultural even though the biological structures which allow for word sounds are natural and located in the body. Indeed Vygotsky (1986) argues that language meanings are, first of all, social before becoming psychological. This does not deny the mental features of language and meaning since, as Chomsky has argued, there must be rational mental structures to provide and generate rational linguistic order in the mind. As we have seen however, earlier in the book, Chomsky is only interested in the inner rational grammatical order of words and not external sociocultural meaning.

On the other hand, we have seen that systemic functional linguistics acknowledges meaning within grammar and we can see this in gendered grammar for example, but this comes from the external social world and does not affect underlying grammatical order. The passive voice, for example, does change word order in terms of subject-object positions, in order to hide agency or to render a statement more authoritative by using an impersonal subject pronoun, however this does not alter the underlying grammar of agency and causality; it simply may leave a gap where the subject should be, and critical discourse analysis begs the question as to the identity of the subject responsible for the action.

It seems then that sociolinguistics and formal linguistics should not be mutually exclusive as in a zero-sum game but should be able to complement each other to account for signification. They simply have different emphases, and the emphasis of sociolinguistics is to look for the origin of meaning in sociocultural context where meaning is both constructed and interpreted by language in context. Saussure himself was interested in the linguistic system as 'langue' but had no interest in language use as 'parole'. This notion of 'parole' as language use is, however, taken up by sociolinguistics and therefore the emphasis in this chapter shifts away from the linguistic system and language structures to language use and the identity of the user of language. Concomitantly there is a parallel continual shift away from the formal linguistic concern with the rational intelligibility of language and towards how users make and interpret meanings. This means that from the user's point of view language is seen as a resource to be drawn upon to convey appropriate meaning according to sociocultural context.

Therefore, an important question is the linguistic resources available to a particular user and groups of users. This of course invokes issues of linguistic opportunity in terms of social categories such as social class, ethnicity, gender, etc. Language in the sociolinguistic paradigm cannot then be separated from its use nor from the identity of the user.

A vital ingredient in enabling the user to impose his/her meaning in language amidst all the other meanings available is the notion of power and I argue that power inserts itself within the relationship between the signified and the signifier in order to shape meaning. Of course, the notion of power is relational and extra linguistic; however, relations of power infiltrate linguistic meanings in order to determine meaning. For example, consider the positive, joyous meaning of the traditional adjective 'gay' which we have already discussed, and which was used extensively in Victorian times to designate 'merry' and 'bright' and often as an adjective to describe vivid colours. Consider at the same time the negative adjectives which had been used in former times to describe 'homosexual', one of which was principally 'queer'. The latter adjective now seems to have been reappropriated in recent times in terms of a positive designation; however, this was not always the case. Social power has displaced these adjectival meanings so that 'gay' now means homosexual, rather than the traditional connotation which is no longer used to designate Victorian style merriment. Interestingly and as already mentioned, the English adjective 'gay' is now used in French to designate same sex relationships. Power in social context is then able to constitute meaning between word-sound-sign and object-idea and to displace old meanings in favour of new ones. Obviously, it takes more than one individual to effect language change and so we need to look to social groups and the power they have to construct ways of speaking to reflect their own identity.

Fairclough (1989) argues that power is such that it is able to create and sustain normalized meaning within ideologically powerful language. This means that meanings become so homogenized that they are taken as common sense, beyond dispute, and therefore normalized. Fairclough describes this as ideological power which is the 'power to project one's practices as universal and common sense' which is a 'significant complement to economic and political power … … …' (1989; p33).

When we refer to language use and language which is expressed by users as a resource for identity and ways of being in the world, sociolinguists refer to discourse since social actors have their own styles of language. Since language is predicated upon social power in the construction of meaning, standard language is seen as a powerful discourse, but still a discourse amongst others except that it has become widespread due to power of such as media and institutions such as education, the law and managerial and bureaucratic practices. At this point we need to examine the notion of discourse since it concerns language in action and is used by both sociolinguists and post-structuralists such as Michel Foucault.

Discourse

To reinforce the notion of discourse as language in use as opposed to language as simply composed of lexis and grammar, Foucault (1972) argues that discourses are not just words and signs but social practices. Foucault states as follows:

> I would like to show that "discourses", in the form in which they can be heard or read, are not, as one might expect, a mere intersection of things and words; an obscure web of things, and a manifest, visible, coloured chain of words; … … … I would like to show with precise examples that in analysing discourses themselves, one sees the loosening of the embrace, apparently so tight, of words and things and the emergence of a group of rules proper to discursive practice.
>
> (1972; p54)

The time now, therefore, is no longer to look inside of language, especially due to the Sausssurean disconnection between the word and the object, since meaning is no longer determined by the word but by the user. So yes, discourse involves words but also other forms of user communication such as gesture, body language, music, styles of dress, etc.

Fairclough's (1989) definition of discourse is not dissimilar from Foucault, in his statement as follows, 'language as social practice determined by social structures' (Fairclough 1989; p17). However, for Fairclough (1992) discourse is one social practice amongst others, whereas for Foucault, discourse is totalizing in that discourse shapes everything we come to know as knowledge as well as social power relations. Many commentators support the view that discourses determine who has the power to speak and who must remain silent and consequently what can be said and what cannot be said (Edwards and Usher 1994; Edwards 1998). In the Foucauldian totalizing model of discourse, discourse has the power to create meaning and consequently knowledge, what is true and what is false, even if this is only local knowledge and consequently this act of securing meaning and therefore knowledge is a very powerful process. This includes the construction of self through knowledge discourses which then shape identity, of which we may be unaware because we are too embedded within the discourse to gain a critical awareness of it. Edwards and Usher (1994) claim that discourse has a silent presence which eludes individuals, and it is for this reason that Fairclough, in his work, calls for critical discourse analysis to raise awareness of individuals' location within discourses which seems invisible because these discourses have become so normalized. Therefore, through critical discourse analysis, Fairclough argues that the individual is not powerless at the mercy of discourse and can stand back from it to gain a critical awareness. We need to, in this regard, examine the external projection of power into discourse which Fairclough refers to as power behind discourse.

Power behind discourse

This refers to participants, knowingly or unknowingly, indexing larger more powerful discourses within more localized social interactions. Individuals may very well draw upon discursive references in the media and incorporate such references in localized social interactions. Gumperz (1999) points out that interpretation of meaning between interlocutors exists at two levels – firstly surface level relating to the immediate sociocultural location and then, secondly and simultaneously, meanings from the wider sociocultural context. The immediate 'ready at hand' meanings trigger the wider meanings and call them into the interaction. Gumperz refers to interactional sociolinguistics, which we will explore later in this chapter, involved in connecting the discourses of the local context to the wider discursive context. The wider discursive context is often taken for granted and used to support the more local discourse. An example of this could be, hypothetically, the man/woman in the street who is interviewed by the media regarding the one per cent recommended rise in salary for health workers proposed by the UK government in March 2021 and updated to three per cent in August 2021. When asked if this rise is sufficient or should be much higher given the front line prominence of nurses and other health workers in the Coronavirus pandemic, the hypothetical person in the street may very well claim that the country cannot afford more than the proposed three per cent increase. The question to be asked in such an interaction is the extent to which the interviewee in the street would have sufficient knowledge of the UK treasury finances and its politico-economic will and capacity for raising taxes to pay for such a rise. The reply that the interviewee in the street gives and the reply an economist might give occupy two different levels of authority, which evoke issues of power. If the economist is the chancellor of public finances with access to the media, his/her level of discourse will have a wider coverage and if unopposed may very well constitute unquestioned background 'knowledge' that becomes so commonsensical that it furnishes the man/woman in the street with a 'ready to hand' response that such a rise cannot be afforded. The issue here is two-fold, firstly access to power within the discourse which in the case of the economist is a powerful expert discourse and secondly power behind the discourse which involves powerful media and institutions to disseminate media statements and render them universal. Edwards (1998) argues that 'Discourses create particular ways of communicating which put forward universal ways of acting.' Discourses therefore offer a particular range of semantic possibilities and exclude others.

An example in an educational context as to how a situated discourse can be empowered by a larger discourse is in the teacher–pupil relationship. Within their classroom interaction the teacher draws upon discourses outside of the particular classroom situation in terms of a readily accessible managerial discourse inside the wider school institution. The institutional discourse in turn draws upon wider governmental educational policy, teacher professional standards and methods monitored by the local inspectorate or advisory teams and also his/her teaching associations, etc. All this represents wider orders of discourse which provide a powerful space at interactional level for the teacher's own discourse. All these powerful discursive influences shape the teacher's discursive practice and render it 'common-sense' and beyond question in a classroom setting, since this constitutes the teacher's professional standards. Notions of critical pedagogy might, nevertheless, think otherwise calling into question this accepted mainstream 'common sense' practice.

Similarly, within the classroom situated interaction, the student draws upon powerful social discourses in his/her cultural location such as family and community and more recently social media platforms. The teacher's discourse type sets the agenda, but the students may not share that agenda and they may draw upon a discourse type which does not share the aims of the school resulting in a conflict between the two discourse types. Fairclough points out that ' ... ... those who hold power at a particular moment have to constantly reassert their power, and those who do not hold power are always liable to make a bid for power' (1989; p68). So, it would be a mistake to view a social situation such as a classroom learning situation as the result of a consensus. The situation visible from the outside may look like consensus but may be the result of a balance of power actually being negotiated and renegotiated inside the social location.

Differences in power can also be seen in the media in the difference between mainstream media and current social media channels. In the former there is much more of an appearance of consensus and difference of opinion in debate is regulated by a moderator in the immediate situation and in the background by a producer who ensures that only a socially accepted range of opinion and language is represented in the production. By contrast social media platforms such as Twitter are much more democratic and interactive, although unregulated with wider norms of acceptable linguistic behaviours and social attitudes. Both types of media are reliant on discourse where the former, in its interaction, draws upon the wider institutional discourse of production teams enforcing standards to manufacture consensus and the latter is simply a minimally regulated platform for heterogeneous discourse, drawing nonetheless on wider societal discourse types. In the traditional television media, there is a clearer and closer relationship between the interactional discourse on the set and the institutional power behind the discourse in programming and production. Discursive consensus is therefore much more likely in the traditional media and visible conflict more prevalent on social media platforms. Power behind the discourse consequently shapes a more hegemonic power within discourse.

Power within discourse

Notions of power within discourse draw upon voices outside particular discursive locations to validate localized discourse. This is evident in academic writing which draws upon widely acknowledged academic authority as a reference to add weight to one's own argument. The voice of one's own discourse then incorporates the voices of powerful others which is a legitimizing force. In the case of academic writing however this is an overt process where references are cited within the text and in reference sections. Failure to acknowledge the voice of others, as a purposeful act, in academic texts is a serious transgression because of a concealment of transparency and a lack of such acknowledgement of the voice of others in taking someone's views as one's own is seen as intellectual theft. However, this is not the case in other areas of unregulated areas of discursive life where voices jostle for position and the more powerful voices take precedence. Evans (2018) refers to competing discourses in schools where powerful socio-economic orders of discourse help create a performance ideology and an internal market within education in the form of league tables. In turn this socio-economic discourse opens up spaces in the curriculum where certain subjects are more favourably promoted over others. Consequently, STEM subjects of science, technology, engineering and maths are considered more important than the arts, music, drama, humanities and even Modern Foreign Languages, because of their economic benefits to the nation.

Indeed, Modern Foreign Languages or MFL occupies an interesting position because, in order to promote it as an important part of the curriculum, practitioners often emphasize its economic value in that one needs to learn and speak a foreign language to sell goods abroad. The MFL pedagogic discourse consequently revolves around the business world and transactional language and runs the risk of becoming instrumentalized in the service of economics (Kramsch 1998). One can see that indeed the languages taught are the languages of historically economic power such as French, German and Spanish as opposed to the community languages of the UK or Central African languages for example. Due to its economic standing in the world Mandarin Chinese has become a feature of many schools MFL curriculum offer, and this is a case in point of economic power creating a discursive rationale for language study.

Often the ideologies around pedagogy and the curriculum are not called into question because, as Hart (2016) argues, the normalization of ideology gradually inserts itself into the beliefs and values of everyday discourse which social participants come to view as perfectly natural.

Economic discourse is not the only ideology which permeates into the curriculum. There are also sociocultural orders of discourse such as liberal democratic values which are reflected in the curriculum in terms of the democracy of student voice and the promotion of lively student debate in particular in the citizenship curriculum and its pedagogy.

Much of what we have said so far in this chapter might seem to imply discursive determinism where the more powerful discourses 'colonize' smaller discourses and that which determines discursive power relates to socioeconomics. Fairclough (1989) certainly takes this view and Tannen (2009) argues that 'When we think we are using language, language is using us' (2009; p303). In fairness however to Fairclough (1992), he does point out that discourse is only one social practice amongst others and acknowledges areas of non-discursive social life which influences us. However, there is not enough emphasis on individual agency and sometimes one wonders whether the individual speaks language or language speaks the individual and this is the age-old debate of free will versus determinism which divides social sciences. Discourses are multiple and competing where the individual has to negotiate between all these competing voices and so consequently the emphasis needs to be more at the level of the individual using discourses as a resource as opposed to regarding discourses as powerful language systems.

Giardiello (2018) argues that 'The socio-cultural context in which young people live is characterized by competing, complementary and divergent values and beliefs provided by parents, school, the consumer society, peer relations and of course the media' (2018; p89). Giardiello argues for the agency of young people being a counter argument against an over deterministic linguistic position, evidenced by young people's engagement in new technologies such as Snapchat, TikTok, Facebook and their creative use of YouTube channels. This implies a multiplicity of identity formation beyond the traditional pillars of School, Community and Family.

Therefore, it may no longer be the case that the identity of one particular social category prevails, and the notion of identity may indeed be multiple identities which diverge according to different subject positions afforded by many sociocultural categories available in social media discourses. Interactional sociolinguists explore identities at the level of individuals in how they both interpret and use discourses as a resource. Ochs (2012) refers to, 'a mindless and imprisoning force of language' (2012; p146) and this description evokes the deterministic force of social categories conveyed in more powerful discourses. She argues that a countervailing force of everyday language is its ability to express the immediacy of being in the world. This is the view of language taken by interactional sociolinguistics exploring how individuals use language to construct the world and to call it into being.

Interactional sociolinguistics

Agency in the use of language is asserting an identity of interpretation. The individual decides what an utterance means at the level of the interaction, taking into account the broader discursive context. I might hear someone ask an interlocutor, 'Are you free now?'. There is a surface level of identity in this utterance which relates to the grammatical structure of the question as opposed to the identity of the interlocutor. This is a grammatical identity in that it is an intelligible question relating to a universal grammar of verb as a state of being with 'to be', subject pronoun, predicate as adjective and time adverb. Chomsky is likely to view this as evidence of a rational mind. However, there is more to an utterance than its grammatical identity as we have to place it in social context. This involves interpretation by social participants making and hearing the utterance. The speaker needs to interpret the context of the event and the personal context of the listener in his/her own interpretation of 'free'. Is sh/e posing the question to someone in terms of availability, asking, for example to meet for coffee or is s/he making an enquiry as to whether the interlocutor is 'released' from physical or judicial constraints, for example from a prison sentence. Therefore, the full identity of the utterance is more than rational intelligibility; it must incorporate the identities of the subject participants. Identity here in sociolinguistics involves interpretation.

Interpretation involves indexicality to a wider discourse because, as Ochs points out, utterances in themselves are incomplete and need to reach out beyond themselves for a more complete meaning. Ochs (2012) describes language as an encounter between personal lived experience and the identity of language as a system and we have witnessed this in the simple question above, between the identity of the question as grammar and the identities of the social participants. Ochs makes the following statement with regard to identities, 'In this perspective, semiotic enactments are temporary unfolding experiences whose configuration at any moment is influenced by the voices, bodies and dispositions of others present and non-present and calculation of the situation at hand' (2012; p153). Language then can be seen as an interplay between lifeworld and system with the concomitant construction of culture as both sociocultural identity as process and also as sociocultural product.

Consequently, we must have simultaneously a regard on what we say as our utterances unfold and in the wider discourse as sociocultural context. There is an interplay simultaneously occurring between these two levels of discourse both as process and product and this comes to us through the notion of heteroglossia.

Heteroglossia

Chouliaraki and Fairclough (1999) refer to Bakhtin's dialectical theory of discourse which posits that discourse does not consist of one unitary voice but of many voices or heteroglossia. In referring to Bakhtin's (1981) ideas, Chouliaraki and Fairclough argue that, '... ... discourse is so to speak internally dialogical, it is "polyphonic", "double-voiced", "double-languaged".' They claim that intertextuality, which is a feature of heteroglossia, is 'the combination in my discourse of my voice and the voice of another.' Mills (2003) states that 'Discourses should not be seen as wholly cohesive, since they always contain within them conflicting sets of statements; for example, the discourse of masculinity cannot be seen as a simple unitary whole' (2003; p64).

An example of the different voices in discourse is evidenced again in education, which we will see is far from being a unitary discourse. The classroom teacher is very likely to draw upon wider management and psychological discourses beyond his/her practitioner discourse in an indexical process where these discourses of, for example, target setting or Vygotsky/Bruner inspired peer group learning, both of which hardly existed historically, have now become integrated into pedagogy. They are now part of a professional practitioner discourse in teaching and yet both strands originate in different areas of social practice which are management and developmental psychology. Each of these constituent areas is likely to be penetrated in turn by other powerful discourses. In the case of school management, this will, as a managerial discourse, be shaped by discourses of advertising and marketing since education in schools and universities is now an internal market influenced by leagues tables and advertising to attract students. Individual student target setting at classroom level contributes to this ideology of performance expressed in advertising and marketing at institutional level. Equally within development psychology opposing developmental discourses exist between Piagetian stages of development where students develop according to pre-existing innate levels tied to age and Vygotskyan zone of proximal development where, with capable peers, one can reach beyond one's unaided understanding irrespective of age. Schools in practice may incorporate both viewpoints in practitioner discourse, however the important point to make is that education is not a unitary discourse, and this is likely to be the case for other discourses which are traversed by powerful voices.

Foucault (1972) takes the notion of discursive power to a much higher level in claiming that knowledge itself is not so much expressed by discourse but created by discourse and power. He states that within discourse, power creates knowledge. Mills (2003), with regard to Foucault, states that 'in producing knowledge one is also making a claim for power' (2003; p69). This would suggest that in making a knowledge claim one is, even to a small degree, wielding power and since this occurs very frequently in sociocultural life, power is indeed very much dispersed throughout society. Further on, Mills (2003) states Foucault's view of power as follows, ' …power is conceptualized as a chain or as a net, which is a system of relations spread throughout society, rather than simply as a set of relations between the oppressed and the oppressor'.

Foucault's notion of discourse and power in terms of knowledge is linked to identity formation in terms of who can speak and who cannot speak and what can be said and what cannot be said. Consequently, agendas for knowledge creation are shaped by the exercise of power and those who exercise power are then able to make statements containing knowledge. However, they can also be called into question by those who contest their power. So power is not a fixed entity to be possessed or not possessed and not then something that one has, but rather something that one does. Wang (2011) points out with regard to identity that 'subjectivity is therefore not something that is ready-made but something that evolves with power/knowledge in its eternal flow' (2011; p153 *Journal of Philosophy of Education*). Discursive identity is then not static but dynamic and productive and so identity like culture is more in a process of becoming rather than an objective product, as individuals move between discourses whilst themselves exercising varying degrees of power.

Identity

This chapter gives us a clearer idea of notions of identity from larger socio-economic and cultural categories of class and gender for example, to more differentiated concepts as individuals act and respond differently in their interactions within these larger discourses. The wider progression of this book journeys from conceptual identity in individuals and language as deterministic and rational, then moving towards social positions in terms of sociocultural categories and then onward towards more individually differentiated identities in discourse with an emphasis on agency and the individual's exercise of power. A concomitant journey has been made in discourse from the construction of culture identity as a product to the ongoing construction of cultures identities as process. Emerging features of identity fit in with Saussurean features of sameness and difference at different levels. Larger categories of language and discourse shape larger categories of identity in terms of grammatical rationality and common sociocultural identities such as gender and class. Yet the more language and discourse are refined into differentiations, the more the categories themselves are differentiated and the more we see individualization in terms of agency. This does not deny the larger categories, but it simply means that these larger categories are only a starting point for identity and not an end result. Saussure himself would argue that a tree is a tree because it resembles other trees in the large category but that when we look closer, we see the differences and the differentiated identities emerging with different names. We are consequently led to consider culture identity both as a larger relatively stable product and as a dynamic process involving agency. Commonality is present as identity in the larger situations which is relatively but not completely stable and at the same time processes of agency would mean that individual linguistic and semiotic behaviours construct differentiated identities within daily actions. The latter may very well come to shape the larger more stable identities over time and so identity formation is a dialectical process between process and product.

This book does not address spiritual identity but there is no reason to suppose that there is any difference in the dialectic between spiritual identities in individuals within their groups and the more fixed identity of the ecclesiastical institution. Sometimes change occurs whereas at other times splinter groups take root and pursue an alternative development. This area of spiritual identity formation could be a possibility of further research for another book.

Identity as linguistic cultural capital

Sociolinguists argue that language use conveys sociocultural identity. They maintain that accent and phraseology are not just a matter of region or city but also a marker of social class and when one explores the theoretical issues around this, one understands why.

Indeed, we all occupy a social position as language users and so language use is not neutral since we all speak in a certain way and have a particular pronunciation. The question is why are some ways of speaking valued socially whilst others are not? Why do newsreaders of whatever TV Channel not present the news or analyse the news with a strong Scouse or Brummie accent? Why is there no Bradford or Manchester English dictionary whereas, as we all know, we have the Oxford or Cambridge English dictionary?

The answer concerns sociocultural and economic power. The answer concerns socio-cultural and economic power in that the powerbase for this in England has historically been in a triangle with the vertices falling on the great medieval cultural, economic and academic centres of Oxford, Cambridge and London, and not Birmingham, Liverpool and Manchester. Therefore, language and culture emanating from these great cultural centres are highly valued and appear to be the prestige language of the intelligentsia.

Bourdieu (1991) criticizes the notion of prestige language such as the 'Queen's English' being more intelligent/cultured than non-standard varieties as 'Misrecognition' or in French 'Méconnaissance'. Bourdieu wrote about language in France which is highly homogenized and regulated by the 'Académie Française' and yet his theories can be extrapolated to other countries. In Spain, it is said that the purest Spanish or Castilian is spoken in the region of Castile around Valladolid and Salamanca, site of the oldest universities in Spain, and by extension cultural power. However social class needs to be factored into this, because even in the centres of cultural power, there will be working class local accents which will be non-standard. So, prestige ways of speaking are not just a matter of geography but also of social class and are valued in such a way because of people's misrecognition. Without this, they would have the same status as any other non-standard accent.

Bourdieu, in his notion of 'misrecognition', says that we are easily taken in or duped by social power and by those who have sociocultural capital and consequently they are viewed as inherently more cultured and intelligent. He argues that this is an illusion, and we can easily become victims of this if we do not cultivate critical awareness. So, language is a marker of sociocultural as well as regional identity. Bourdieu (1991) views linguistic and cultural identity as a symbolic capital much in the same way as finance and this is validated by the power of prestige embedded within social class which may mean that those with prestige accents and pronunciation are more readily listened to whereas those with regional and social class-based accents may be ignored.

Conclusion

There is a danger in overstating individual agency in the construction of identity which as Foucault points out is promoted by neoliberal discourse. Spohrer et al. (2018) underline Foucault's view that this discourse type encourages the individual to construct him/herself as an entrepreneur as opposed to a more traditional discourse where the worker exchanges her/his labour for money. Spohrer et al. argue that the entrepreneurial view of the individual entails individual self-control as opposed to being controlled and so notions of discipline become internalized within the individual. Why would this view of individualized agency seem to be contentious? The answer is that the individual is expected to take control of his/her own agency as a personal project regardless of social disadvantage and so the more this self-management discourse is promoted the more the wider socio-economic discourse containing social injustice and disadvantage is exonerated from moral responsibility. So, the onus is shifted onto the individual to lift him/herself out of social deprivation and poverty and of course not to rely on the state for help. This particular discourse of the entrepreneurial individual is seen in the schools' curriculum where school business studies projects involve mini-enterprise week where students set up their own businesses in groups or pairs to market and sell products with profits going to the school's chosen charity. Many young people now in the world of commerce set up their own 'start-ups' rather than becoming employees, and consequently work from home or rent office spaces alongside other 'start-up' entrepreneurs.

This discourse of enterprise to encourage self-reliance and agency may very well be taken up enthusiastically and benefit many people but it nonetheless shows how educational discourse can be colonized by larger socioeconomic discourse to manufacture entrepreneurial agency.

It must not be forgotten that in spite of an entrepreneurial cultural discourse to encourage people to take responsibility for themselves, within the discourse, language type and genre still contains a symbolic capital which legitimizes some language types over others. There is still then a linguistic cultural identity within discourse where standard language exerts dominance over non-standard language and received pronunciation or Queen's English in the UK provides legitimacy to what is said. Bourdieu (1991) sees this linguistic cultural identity as crucial in gaining symbolic power and access to cultural and material resources.

However extensive one regards the notion of discourse as constitutive of social structure, power is integral to this constitution. If, in a Foucauldian model, discourse constitutes society itself through discursive formations which construct knowledge from what can be said and what cannot be said, and who can speak and who cannot speak, then power runs through all social structures, even to the identity of one's being in the world; identity being then not who one is but what one can do and say.

For Fairclough (1989, 1992), discourse is one social practice amongst others and, in a model of capitalist society, expresses economic relations in three concentric layers so that the outer layer represents the socio-economic orders of discourse, the middle layer represents the institutional discourse types such as schools and the inner layer, the interactive situational discourse. Therefore, the power in the smaller situational discourse is driven by the power of the wider socio-economic discourse.

It is therefore insufficient to state that the identity of the individual and his/her language lies only within his/her construction of words, phrases and utterances, along with his/her standard or non-standard accent and dialect without taking into account the full context of societal discourse. This is because the individual resides within power structures which shape her/his access to knowledge and also language use as social and symbolic capital. In this regard I use the notion of 'shapes' rather than 'determines' since, as we will see in the next chapter, social actors in their groups act in different ways in relation to social forces in terms of the way in which they interpret and make their own meanings within their own linguistic and discursive identities.

The next chapter will explore this latter individual agency in identity formation, set within the notion of inter-subjectively constituted identities.

6

Intersubjectivity

In this chapter we explore individual agency within intersubjective identities, where in Bakhtinian dialogism (Bakhtin 1981) and heteroglossia, our discursive utterances contain the voices, often powerful, of others. The impact on identity is in fact identities in the plural coming out of multiple voices that exist in the ongoing threads of our daily discourses. We learn indeed that the voices of others that exist within our own identity belong to the social world as identities that shape us as we traverse and become involved in different social situations. I think it is true to say that in different social situations as, for example, when we move from formal to informal and back again, we change our language register and consequent subjectivity. In Chapter 7 on narrative identities, we will explore how the notion of the subjective self relates to ongoing narrative identity as we encounter the various forms of alterity or the 'other'.

We explore, in this chapter, the social foundations of language as proposed by Vygotsky and, although Bakhtin and Vygotsky both view meaning and identity as originating in the social world, there is a difference of emphasis between them as we shall see in the next section. We conclude the chapter with a section on performative language which introduces the notion of power in language, leading to language as action as opposed to description.

Vygotsky and Bakhtin, two Russian linguistic thinkers: A comparative view

Vygotsky was one of Russia's major thinkers with regard to language development in children and young people. Unlike Piaget, Vygotsky did not view the individual as influenced by inner genetic stages of development but instead more by his/her social context. For this he is known as being a social constructivist due to the social nature of language, identity and cognitive development.

For Vygotsky the individual internalizes language and meanings from the social environment in a process of individualization through inner speech. The inner speech belongs to the individual's own unique psychology originating from a set of communal meanings and resulting in a distinction between inner speech and the social identity of external speech. Vygotsky states as follows that 'Inner speech is speech for oneself; external speech is for others' (Thought and Language, 1986; p225).

Vygotsky contends that inner speech is preceded by egocentric speech in the development of the child but that this fades out at school age to be gradually replaced by inner speech. Egocentric speech is actually verbalized by the child and can be heard in its accompaniment to the child's play or other activities, whereas inner speech is particular to the child's individual identity as a purely psychological rather than linguistic phenomenon. Vygotsky argues that 'Egocentric speech has no function in the child's realistic thinking or activity – it merely accompanies them. And since it is an expression of egocentric thought, it disappears with the child's egocentrism' (1986; p227). We notice that Vygotsky refers to the individual in terms of a unitary identity as he talks about the child's inner world, and we will see later on in this section how this differs from Bakhtin's notion of the individual's multiple identities where the notion of a unitary identity is shot through with the identities of others through the language of others in a dialogic chain. The Bakhtinian narrative of multiple identities or voices does not in any way undermine the work of Vygotsky but rather complements it. Both linguistic thinkers draw upon the social nature of language in the construction of identity (individual for Vygotsky and intersubjective for Bakhtin), but their focus of analysis occurs at different levels. Vygotsky focuses on the objective process or mechanism of social language becoming psychologized within the individual whereas Bakhtin focuses on how the language of others penetrates the identity of individuals within intersubjective social interaction. Bakhtin's key notion is then intersubjective identity whereas Vygotsky's emphasis is on how social language becomes individualized within the psychology of the individual. Vygotsky posits a dialectical relationship between thought and word as follows, 'The relation of thought to word is not a thing but a process, a continual movement back and forth from thought to word and from word to thought. Thought is not merely expressed in words, it comes into existence through them' (Vygotsky 1986; p218). Thoughts are then not just carried by words; they are also contained in them. Vygotsky points out that, 'Thought undergoes many changes as it turns into speech. It does not merely find expression in speech; it finds its reality and form' (1986; p219). Further on Vygotsky states, 'The relation of thought and word cannot be understood in all its complexity, without a clear understanding of the psychological nature of inner speech' (1986; p224). Vygotsky outlines a process of external social speech becoming egocentric speech as an accompaniment to the child's activity which then disappears to be replaced by inner speech which is no longer dependent on the socially recognizable word. Vygotsky states as follows, 'The decreasing vocalization of egocentric speech denotes a developing abstraction from sound, the child's new faculty to "think words" instead of pronouncing them' (1986; p230).

Vygotsky comes to regard inner speech as a new speech function disconnected as such from complete words with abbreviations, agglutinations of several word morphemes to form compounds, predicates preceding subjects, where the predicate has more psychological impact than the subject. Inner speech becomes individualized, psychologized within the individual and consequently incomprehensible to others were it to become externalized. One word in inner speech could indeed represent several words in external social speech. Eventually thought becomes pure and not at all dependent on words but rather upon psychological motivation. Vygotsky states that the development of verbal thought runs a course 'from motive that engenders a thought to the shaping of the thought, first in inner speech then in meanings of words and finally in words' (1986; p257). Vygotsky's emphasis appears to be more on the psychological aspect of language and linguistics whereas Bakhtin, as we will see, lies much more on an interactional, intersubjective applied linguistics.

Bakhtin follows the same general notion as Vygotsky of the individual's language and identity being constituted from the social to the individual although Bakhtin's line of this development is not of one social voice but of many. Bakhtin views individuals' identities as intersubjectively constituted since they are always entangled within a network of voices and identities. He claims that 'in the everyday speech of any person living in society, no less than half (on the average) of words uttered by him will be someone else's words (consciously someone else's), transmitted with varying degrees of precision and impartiality (or more precisely partiality)' (Bakhtin 1981). I think that added to this are the words of others that we process and transmit unconsciously. However, this should come as no surprise because we are born into a language which is not of our making but rather the making of others. Over the course of our lives, we then borrow words and their meanings from a common linguistic pool either belonging to our own community social group or that of the wider society and we use these words as though they were our own. The name he gives to this is heteroglossia where we speak with the voices of others. Shotter (1993) refers to Bakhtin's claim that 'we have no internal sovereign territory of our own' (1993; p382) meaning that unlike Vygotsky's position of a unitary subjectivity, Bakhtin's view is that individual identity is always populated by other people's voices. Therefore, we need to refer to intersubjective identities as opposed to a single unitary identity. Furthermore, language is never neutral because it always reflects someone's point of view and social position. Although Bakhtin does not explicitly mention power, he implicitly evokes power in his reference to 'forces' as follows:

> Unitary language constitutes the theoretical expression of the historical processes of linguistic unification and centralization, an expression of the centripetal forces of language. A unitary language is not something given but is always in essence posited – and at every moment of its linguistic life it is opposed to the realities of heteroglossia. But at the same time, it makes its real presence felt as a force for overcoming this heteroglossia, imposing specific limits, guaranteeing a certain maximum of mutual understanding and crystalizing into a real, although relative unity – the unity of the reigning conversations (everyday) and literary language. 'correct language' (Bakhtin 1981; p270).

There is then a powerful social force holding a common language and identity together as unitary, preventing the dispersal of language and identity towards a natural diversification. Bakhtin underlines this unificatory force as follows, 'A common unitary language is a system of linguistic norms' and these norms are, 'the generative forces of linguistic life, forces that struggle to overcome the heteroglossia of language, forces that unite and centralize verbal – ideological thought … …' (1981; pp270-1). For Bakhtin then the internalization of language and concomitant identities is more than just a mechanical process of the movement from the social to the individual, it is indeed very political and very ideological where social forces attempt to constrain individuals into a 'norm' of language and identity. Bakhtin argues, '… a unitary language gives expression to forces working toward concrete verbal and ideological unification and centralization, which develop in vital connection with the processes of sociopolitical and cultural centralization' (1981; p271).

However, Bakhtin argues that, nevertheless, linguistic diversification is a natural dynamic and that there is a constant opposing movement between diversification in language, identity and culture on the one hand and, on the other, unification or, in other words, between centrifugal and centripetal forces respectively. In his words, he states, 'Alongside the centripetal forces, the centrifugal forces of language carry on their uninterrupted work; alongside verbal-ideological centralization and unification, the uninterrupted processes of decentralization and disunification go forward' (1981; p272).

Consequently, even at the level of the individual, utterances themselves are simultaneously subject to those opposing forces of dispersal and standardization. Bakhtin argues that 'Every conversation is full of transmissions and interpretations of other people's words' (1981; p338). We can then see how Vygotsky and Bakhtin both draw upon the social world for language and identity, although in different ways and at different levels. Vygotsky's emphasis is on a social monoglossic or monolinguistic process and here the key element is the mechanism of internalization itself. Bakhtin does not undermine this process but expands and refines it towards intersubjectivity. He looks at the content of the identity rather than the process of internalization and argues that the content of identity has a natural propensity towards diversification or dispersal but that what holds identity together as unitary is the ideologically social force of standardization. Bakhtin does not mention power explicitly and we really have to wait for Foucault in the late twentieth century to highlight the interrelation between power, knowledge, identity and discourse. Bakhtin does, however, refer to the networks and chains of language individuals are engaged in and does refer to discourse to reflect the ideological positions from which they are speaking. He states that 'The topic of a speaking person takes on quite another significance in the ordinary ideological workings of our consciousness, in the process of assimilating our consciousness to the ideological world. The ideological becoming of a human being, in this view, is the process of selectively assimilating the words of others' (Bakhtin 1981; p341). Different discursive utterances then form a network of heteroglossia shaping the linguistic contributions of others within chains of dialogue, helping to form ideological identities from many voices where some are more powerful than others.

Bakhtin and subcultural language

For Bakhtin (1981), language exists on the cusp of Self and the Other. Language predates our existence, it is not ours; it is, in itself, an embodiment of the Other, and yet, as already mentioned, we borrow it from the common pool and attempt to make it our own, imbuing it with our own subject position meanings. This chapter is crucial in the book because it represents the two forces of language, which this book attempts to reconcile, which are the simultaneously occurring of both the centralizing force and also the force of dispersal and differentiation. Bakhtin, who names these respectively the centripetal force and the centrifugal force, applies these opposing forces to culture in general. This means that in language, at least, there is a core of commonality and at the same time, a marginalization where language becomes the property of different groups and or ethnicities with different ideological meanings. Bakhtin (1981) states that 'Every concrete utterance of a speaking subject serves as a point where centrifugal as well as centripetal forces are brought to bear. The process of centralization and decentralization of unification and disunification intersect in the utterance' (1981; p272). Bakhtin reinforces this double action as follows, 'Every utterance participates in the unitary language in its centripetal forces and tendencies and at the same time partakes of social and historical heteroglossia' (1981; p272).

We see that there are urban dialects such as Rap language and Verlan in France that have an anti-establishment position and yet they derive their basic structure from the common linguistic pool and therefore carry an inner linguistic commonality. However, at the level of lexis, meanings and spellings change so that their communication is only readily understood within a particular culture. Verlan, a French urban dialect in particular, reverses the syllables in its pronunciation and spellings and incorporates words from Eastern Europe and North Africa from where many of the dialect users originate. Jackson and Amvela (2007) state that subcultures exist that generate their own vocabulary. They state, 'This vocabulary then becomes a badge of membership of the sub-culture; you learn and use the appropriate words to prove that you are a member and in order to associate with other members' (2007; p155). Such subcultural slang, according to Jackson and Amvela, occurs in the criminal underworld and they cite many examples of vocabulary relating to prison such as 'can, chokey, clink, cooler, nick, peter, slammer, stir' and being sentenced to prison as 'bang up, do bird, go down, be inside, do porridge'. Within criminal dialect they also cite the slang used for the police as, 'the filth, the fuzz, the pigs' (2007; pp156-7).

Many of these words become known beyond their particular subculture and enter the standard language and become used wore widely. There is then some intersubjectivity in the way we might position ourselves for example if we were to refer to the police as 'the filth'. It could lead to a question of where we stand in relation to the police by the simple usage of this negatively loaded word and if we were to combine this with other criminal subcultural language, we might be positioning ourselves or playing a role part in a particular anti-establishment way even if we had no criminal convictions. Therefore, through language we can take on different subject positions and, in this sense language and identity are intersubjective, binding together those who belong because they know the language and at the same time excluding others who do not know the language. In this respect urban dialects and indeed prestige standard language and pronunciation as well as regional dialect serve as a marker not only of belonging but also of non-belonging and exclusion.

Bakhtin (1981) argues for an intersubjective notion of language through heteroglossia. Heteroglossia, as already mentioned, means that one's utterance contains the voice of the other because it exists in a chain of utterances involving interlocutors. In modern terms this could visibly resemble a Twitter thread where there are many voices contributing to a constructed and often contested reality. A Twitter utterance may contain references to the previous interlocutor and may reuse his/her words to make a fresh statement which is then picked up and interpreted by others further along the Twitter thread. This would be analogous to how Bakhtin sees language in operation. Indeed, when we speak, we refer to what has already been stated either in person or more generally in the media. Our voice is then not totally our own. Bakhtin claims as follows that 'The authentic environment of an utterance, the environment in which it lives and takes shape is dialogized heteroglossia, anonymous and social but simultaneously concrete, filled with specific content and accented as an individual utterance' (1981; p272). There is a commonality in an utterance which contains its intelligibility and makes for understanding in its transmission but at the same time it is 'accented' with the subject position of the user. The social nature of language means that the language we hear is not neutral since it comes to us from social participants and is saturated with the purposes and intentions of other people. The Other may be powerful in terms of the media at its disposal with a wide network of transmission to project influential voice to a wide range of listening, viewing and reading audiences. Bakhtin states that 'there are no "neutral" words and forms of words, and forms that belong to no-one, language has been completely taken over, shot through with intentions and accents' (1981; p293).

Consequently, words are always someone's words as Bakhtin once again says, 'All words have the "taste" of a profession, a genre, a tendency, a party, a particular work, a particular person, a generation, an age group, the day and the hour. Each word tastes of the context and contexts in which it has lived its socially charged life' (1981; p293).

Dialogism

For Bakhtin, all language is dialogic and there is a very simple logic to explain this. We utter words to be heard and even if we utter these words to ourselves, we are indeed speaking to our inner selves. When we write, we do this to be read. Both Bakhtin and Vygotsky hold the view that language is social and so when we speak or write, we are doing this for an audience, even if this is an imaginary one or even our future selves in diary entries. In many if not most cases we anticipate a response at some point even if many months or years in the future and again this may be ourselves as our own audience in times to come for those who maintain diaries or autobiographical notes. If we are using present-day social media such as Twitter, we expect a fairly immediate response and even, based upon positive responses, a sizeable number of followers. Twitter users with hundreds of thousands of followers can claim to be 'influencers'. Because of this dialogic communication, our utterances intended to be read by others, take account of their possible responses and to some extent we may construct utterances in anticipation of the responses. To this extent our speech and writing are shaped by the anticipated responses of others. The intersubjectivity is evident in that the speaker requires a hearer and the hearer requires a speaker or in the case of writing, a reader. This is why we switch on the television or read a book, newspaper or social media. The two ends of communication are then intertwined and depend upon each other.

The dialogism is forever ongoing because the speaker projects a meaning into the world beyond the physical phonemes of the words. The meaning needs to be acknowledged for completion. It is then interpreted by the listener to give a fuller meaning to the original utterance which is then reinterpreted by the original speaker in succeeding utterances. This line of utterance, interpretation by the interlocutor, reinterpretation by the original speaker or other speaker(s) followed by further utterances and interpretations provide the rationale for ongoing dialogism and create the space for intersubjectivity.

If the speaker or writer had no listener or reader, could meaning ever be complete? From a dialogic point of view the answer would have to be no. The utterances must have a response for the completion of meaning. The reader completes the meaning of a book by bringing meaning to its fulfilment, by providing a fuller or wider interpretation. An uttered meaning without a response is really only a potential meaning as it is only partial without an interpretation for a more complete meaning. Even the person who keeps a diary, making notes about his/her life and self, does not have completion in meaning because, in the course of time, s/he will be, arguably, a different person in terms of identity, since identity is ongoing and, may well reread the diary entry with a more developed or different identity. He/she may then feel a need to update or perhaps mentally critique what has been written some time ago. Even if the person does not make a revision, it might well be the case that the person says, 'Well this is what I felt back then' almost as though she/he is a different person now. It could be that there is no desire to revise or critique what has been written but this depends upon the time that has elapsed since the written entry. An elderly person rereading a youthful account of him/herself must surely be acknowledging that he/she is no longer quite the same person due to an ongoing and developing identity over the years.

The outcome of this is that there is no finality to meaning or identity because of interpretation and reinterpretation continuing and ongoing into the future. Interlocutors in dialogic situations, furthermore, use the voices of others, reinterpret the subject positions of others and so dialogue is shot through with the meanings and voices of others due to heteroglossia. Consequently, the notion of an individual unitary and isolated identity has to be called into question.

This has an interesting implication for foreign language learning because when the learner speaks the language of the other with the accent, grammar and lexis of the other, the learner is beginning to take on the cultural identity of the other alongside his/her own present cultural identity. Intersubjectivity is then a constant interplay between self and other where the boundaries of identity are blurred and indistinct.

The spirituality of dialogism

Perlina (1984) refers to Martin Buber as framing dialogism in spiritual terms in terms of the 'I' and 'Thou' relationship with reference to truth. Buber and Bakhtin subscribe to the view that truth does not reside in the head of one individual but 'is born between people in their communal search' (1984; pp9–10). For Buber, the truth arises from the 'I', 'Thou' relationship since the 'I', 'Thou' is at the basis of all relations and is spiritual because the relationship with the Other is of the same nature as the relationship with God. Charmé (1977) points out that ' … he (Buber) believes that a personal relationship with God is of the same fundamental nature as an authentic relation to one's fellow human' (1977; p161). Therefore, for Buber the dialogic nature of human relations specifically addresses an ethical intersubjectivity replacing 'I'/'It' with 'I'/'Thou', thereby replacing objectified human relations with caring, ethical relationships addressing the Other. This is based on the perception and appreciation of the other person as unique in him/herself as opposed to being instrumentalized in any way. It is designed to be a full acknowledgement of alterity or the Other, where 'I' and 'Thou' are construed in a reciprocity, each echoing the other. Here the other is reflected in oneself, the 'I' and 'Thou' are interrelated yet different, rendered different by the subject pronouns without which there would be a continuous undifferentiated reality with indistinct boundaries between the two identities; yet nevertheless related because the other of 'thou' can only exist from the view of the self or 'I', and so without 'I' there is no 'other' or 'thou'.

Bakhtin and Buber show then that identity is not individually isolated and unitary but contains a shared subjectivity and we construct the world with our understandings of the world in continual dialogue.

How we come to do this in the first place is the subject area of social constructivism and the work of Vygotsky demonstrates how such intersubjectivity begins in very early childhood when children first begin to use language.

Vygotsky's social constructivism

The basis of intersubjectivity is that all language, for Vygotsky (1986), is social before becoming individual. Language becomes internalized over the course of individual development and so begins the process of the social construction of self which leads us eventually to the dialogism of Bakhtin. There is a continuous reality between the young infant, others and the rest of the world that only become differentiated through the internalization of words and their meanings. Before becoming individualized the socially based word-meanings must enter into the cognitive areas of the young. Vygotsky (1986) refers to a precognitive linguistic state before the age of 18 months–2 years where the child's speech is instinctual. The phonemes are biological responses rather than social because the linguistic and cognitive areas of mind have not yet entered into a connectivity. Vygotsky's position is that language and thought originate in separate areas of the mind and these areas need to come together to produce individualized meaningful words. When the words enter into a cognitive relationship in the mind, they have pre-established social meanings and are then processed by the child. Vygotsky shows that the developing consciousness of the child as s/he processes word-meaning occurs through inner speech.

Before consciousness the child is unable to fully appreciate the independent existence of others and is unable to understand his/her own separate existence from others in the world. It is the operation of language and its internalization which enable this to happen. This happens, according to Vygotsky, through egocentric speech where the child is able to accompany his/her actions with a commentary in order to represent to him/herself problems and obstacles to be overcome in activities. Egocentric speech, as mentioned in an earlier section, is then integral to the development of the young child's awareness which, for Vygotsky, eventually becomes inner speech linking up external and internalized language. Vygotsky states, 'Egocentric speech emerges when the child transfers social collaborative forms of behaviour to the sphere of inner personal psychic functions' (1986; p35).

Through egocentric and then ongoing inner speech, the child internalizes social relations very early on in life as Vygotsky points out, 'In our conception, the true direction of the development of thinking is not from the individual to the social but from the social to the individual' (1986; p36).

In the work of Bakhtin (1981) we see how intersubjectivity works in dialogism and heteroglossia with an emphasis on agency as part of this internal/external interrelationship, and, with Vygotsky we learn how this intersubjectivity originates in the child in terms of the internalization of social language, in an internal/external relationship between the personal and the social.

In Vygotsky's (1978) concept of the Zone of Proximal Development, we see how conceptual development and learning are also essentially social rather than individual as in Piaget's Stages of Development. Vygotsky shows how conceptual development in a learning process involves others who may be teachers but also 'capable peers'. The capable peer or teacher bridges the gap between the child's own current understanding and a more advanced understanding in an area where the child left alone would not be able to progress beyond his/her own conceptual reach. Without the language and sign of others, this gap could not be crossed and so development is indeed constructed through the language of others. However, Vygotsky also says that the relations between higher mental functions were at one time real relations among people. This implies that learning involves power relations where the words which have control over mental functions also represent power that exists relationally in the learning situation. Vygotsky argues that originally the word was a command to action but that now that the word has become separated from action itself in many cases, it still retains the function of command over behaviour. There is then a performative element to language and Vygotsky argues that we only become ourselves through others. So, in the construction of cognition, in the Zone of Proximal Development for example, with the participation of capable peers, the performative element in language arises from the interrelations with others in the learning situation. It can then be argued that when we are in a learning situation, we learn skills, concepts and facts and alongside this, behaviours, from the internalization of power relations within the learning context. Even when we are alone, it could be argued that we manage our thoughts and behaviour through the social language of others that we have internalized. The fact of language, either internal or external as integral to behaviour and action, where the word calls a state of being into existence, contains elements of performative language which rely heavily on intersubjectivity and shared meanings.

Austin (Longworth 2011) saw that language was more than Wittgenstein's view of it being only concerned with truth statements. The notion of power in language suggested by Vygotsky is more developed in Foucault (1972) and this enables the transfer of uttered or written words of intersubjectivity into states of being and action and as we shall see later into claims for knowledge itself.

Performative language

Austin's (Longworth 2011) examples of performative language are statements where an individual's authority or conferred authority declares a situation to be the case, for example where a minister of religion declares a couple to be husband and wife and from that moment, they indeed become a married couple. A university has the authority to confer through a verbal and written declaration that the undergraduate is now a graduate, accompanied by the symbols and signs of academic dress and certificate. In criminal law a judge following a guilty verdict has the authority to declare the guilt of the defendant and verbally announce a prison sentence. This announcement passes into action and is indeed an integral part of the action. Such active language needs certain conditions for the action to be triggered. These have to be a shared understanding of the language if the language is to be mutually understood as integrally connected to the action as a cause–effect and there also has to be a mutually recognized authority behind the language. There are of course areas where these conditions are not met, even in learning situations as mentioned above, where for example in a school classroom, the teacher's authority is not always a shared discourse with the pupils because the pupils may well have more identification with discourses from outside the classroom. Instructions from the teacher may then go unheeded and Vygotsky's Zone of Proximal Development fall on deaf ears. Contrary to this however, a soldier who is a volunteer has signed a contract to obey orders and in this case the sergeant's command is fully integrated to the ensuing action.

Austin (Longworth 2011) divides language into descriptive statements and performative statements or constatives and performatives, respectively. Constatives are the true–false statements that we see in Wittgenstein (1999). These are according to Austin, locutionary statements. Performatives confer a state of being which Austin refers to as illocutionary whereas he refers to statements describing the consequences of a performative statement as perlocutionary. Austin, being an analytical philosopher, is analysing language into its component parts. Foucault coming from a different tradition focuses not so much on language in itself but on language and discourse tied to underlying notions of power. So, to make a statement function and exist in the world there has to be power behind it and individual words and sentences therefore reside within discourses of power. Foucault does not make a distinction between descriptive statements and performative statements because for him a description already has a performative element in the judgement it makes. For example, in education a descriptor for students' work might be 'A' grade or 'D' grade and Marshall (1999) points out that such grading becomes more than description because it has a performative element in turning the student into an 'A' grade or a 'D' grade student. For Foucault, this is performative because it is constitutive of the construction of the individual through power. Therefore, one can argue that performative language often masquerades as descriptive language due to the power of those who are able to make judgemental descriptions on others.

Conclusion

In this chapter we have journeyed along a path towards intersubjectivity by arguing that language and identity are shared social phenomena. Vygotsky shows us the mechanics of the origins of social language and how it becomes individualized and, along with this language development, the concomitant conceptual identity development that accompanies it.

Bakhtin allows us to see the intersubjectivity in operation through dialogized heteroglossia where language and utterance exist in a continual thread of unfinished interpretations going forward into the future in a search for completion.

Austin introduces us to the notion of language as being performative and not just describing true and false situations as do Wittgenstein's constative statements.

Crucially Foucault introduces the notion of power for even a word, phrase or sentence to carry meaning where all language carries with it the power to produce an effect, even to the point of establishing true and false within claims for knowledge. Bakhtin's notion of dialogized heteroglossia reveals through intersubjectivity, the connectedness of our identity with others and further to this, especially with the consideration of Foucault's notion of power, we see the dangers of intersubjectivity in the presence of the power of performative language.

The next chapter will explore what impact intersubjectivity, meanings and power have on identity in how individuals construct their own narratives for identity and then allow themselves to be positioned or are positioned within narratives of identity. Indeed, how individuals negotiate their identity narratives within the age-old polarizations of free will and determinism will be a theme running through the next chapter.

7

Narrative Identities

Introduction

This chapter explores the notion of the construction of narrative identity through language and sign. The main focus is on Ricoeur as the seminal thinker to propose the concept of narrative identity as the way in which individuals attempt to make sense of the disparate and seemingly unrelated life situations which they experience. They seek to achieve coherence through constructing a life story much like a CV. However, in doing so, there is a risk of suppressing or marginalizing other meanings which perhaps do not fit in as appropriate to such an overarching narrative. This risks leaving the narrator as a hero of a fiction or illusory narrative with little grounding in reality.

Ricoeur

Ricoeur's dilemma is how to balance the relationship between 'idem' and 'ipse' where 'idem' is Sameness and 'Ipse' is 'Selfhood' open to the future and in a state of becoming. Van den Hengel (1994) states as follows, 'In the narrative there is an interaction of the self that, on the one hand, maintains an identity of constancy (a self that remains the same, hence "sameness"), with a self that, on the other hand, projects itself into the future and commits itself to chance and transformation, a self that is not yet but becomes in the "kept word" which Ricoeur calls "ipseity"' (1994; p3). Individual identity is then constituted in this dialectical interface between the sameness of 'idem' and the selfhood of becoming in 'ipse'. So, self that is constructed in the narrative to attain to coherence is, ironically, penetrated by difference and may well struggle to maintain its unity. This is an ever-present dilemma due to our use of language in the statements we make, in the present which project to the future, stating our intentions and our promises. Intentions and promises reflect an identity of potential becoming which has not yet happened and yet this may well impact upon our coherent identity of sameness in terms of who we could become. Therefore, we cannot help but be open to future possibilities of an identity of becoming by our linguistic acts delivered in the present. This is indeed an 'Otherness' of future potentiality. The result announces the possibility of change due to a developing identity where the narrative identity is still recognizable but is developed in its forward movement into the future by the possibilities of becoming, especially more so when these future identity possibilities become realized in the present and become incorporated into the narrative. This ongoing development of narrative identity is however not so straightforward as Sheerin (2009) points out as follows, 'If we tell a series of self-narratives, each interlinking, each a fresh story and each a development, a fresh draft, and if each narrative provides "discordant concordance" then what is the relation between one self-narrative and the next … ….?' (2009; p41). Sheerin goes on to ask if a metanarrative needs to be constructed to maintain an overall coherence. Sheerin argues that for Ricoeur the self is a construction to resolve these discordant issues between the sameness of 'idem' identity and the discordances that alterity or otherness brings to bear in the future 'becoming' or in the otherness encountered between the self and the other of intersubjectivity.

Alterity or Otherness is therefore a discordance that needs to be resolved and yet at the same time it presents an openness in encountering the alterity of the future and also the alterity of others in intersubjectivity.

The problem for Ricoeur is that alterity disrupts the narrative identity of sameness into which it inserts possibilities of identity, but which do not possess the substance and the ontology of being which characterizes sameness. So where is the ontological grounding of alterity as a possibility for the identity of becoming? Van den Hengel states that 'In the dialectic of sameness and ipseity, only sameness and not ipseity, can be linked with Being as substance. Is there an ontology for selfhood where the self is not in danger of being reduced to a "something?"' (1994; p4 'Paul Ricoeur's "*Oneself as Another*" and Practical Theology' – John Van den Hengel). In other words where is the guarantee in identity as becoming?

Ricoeur's response to the lack of grounding in the possibilities of becoming lies in the attestation of action which is the belief in Being's commitment to action. Action then becomes the ontology of transforming becoming into Being. Van den Hengel states that 'Sameness is linked to an ontology of being as substance. Ipseity or selfhood must be linked to the ontology of being as act/potency' (1994; p5).

Consequently, Ricoeur's response to the idem/ipse dichotomy of narrative is to ground such narratives in ethical action and so we have the concept of alterity or the Other to whom narrative in action should be a response. Ricoeur talks of one's identity in language as responding to alterity in the other without whom we would have no narrative anyway because our speech or writing needs a listener or reader, as we mentioned in the last chapter; it needs the 'Other', an acknowledgement of intersubjectivity.

Chapter 6's discussion of Bakhtin has allowed us to refer to heteroglossia in this chapter due to the notion that all we speak or write exists in an interwoven thread with the other. So self and other can be conceptualized as interwoven and Sayegh (2008) refers to cultural hybridity to bridge the binary opposition between self and other since the drawback to narrative identity vis-à-vis alterity is the danger that expansion of identity towards the other risks a colonization of alterity. We need then to deconstruct narrative identity without discarding it, to realize that, in the act of deconstruction, Sameness does contain the Other. Apparent sameness in narrative identity may be a useful tool to create coherence, however it should also be seen as an overarching construction that may marginalize identities of alterity or conceal identities that are not appropriate for a given circumstance. In the next Part Four and particularly Chapter 8, we attempt to deconstruct the hegemony of narrative identities to reveal difference in intersubjectivity rather than to uncritically accept a prevailing and possibly constraining sameness of identity.

Signs

We spoke briefly of sign in the last chapter where Foucault (1972) stated that language prior to the Enlightenment was looked upon in the same way as a natural sign such as the movement of the planets, plants or natural elements. Natural signs were seen as marks left on the face of the earth by the Divine for humans to have some knowledge of the existence of God. Indeed, written language in the Middle Ages consisted mainly of religious and biblical texts. In modern times however, signs are seen as semiotic constructions which communicate beyond the physical materiality of the sign-object itself. Commercial signs and logos are an example of this. Religious signs also have this semiotic exteriority although believers would hold to the notion of, for example, Christian signs as having an interior life. So, a crucifix and the Host in the Divine Exposition are worshipped for their interior nature as signs as well as being acknowledged for their exterior semiotic nature.

Nevertheless signs, in terms of semiotics, are constructed as identities. As semiotics are social in nature, a sign can have more than one meanings according to how it is constructed as a cultural narrative. The Christian cross or crucifix can be an outward sign of faith but also it can be a fashion statement with no particular faith content. It is in this context that language and signs are open to interpretation in the construction of narrative of identities. Ullin (2005) refers to Ricoeur's contention that nature itself, as an object of human knowledge, is a construction, culturally constituted within discourse. Of course, this position would leave no room at all for the interiority of the sign since everything is seen as socioculturally constructed. It can be argued that once the one-to-one connection was broken between the natural sign and the natural world or the divine, interiority was lost since signs were subsequently seen as human constructions.

This would suggest that we have no direct knowledge of the natural world beyond our linguistic and semiotic constructions. This echoes the writings of Kant in the Critique of Pure Reason, where he contends that we can have no knowledge of the world beyond our perception. This world beyond perception, he calls the noumenon and of which, according to Wittgenstein in his work on language in the Tractatus, 'we cannot speak'.

Ullin (2005) states that 'meanings are therefore not fixed but dynamic and constantly changing' (2005; p887). This is because language and sign are, as I have argued, not grounded in nature and, as human social constructions, are able to evolve as meanings develop within language. Meanings also change from one culture to another. For example, the hand gesture forming a circle with the forefinger and thumb and the rest of the fingers raised means excellent in American culture whereas in French culture its meaning is of zero worth or useless.

Notions of identity divide into the idea, on the one hand of an 'essentialist' identity which projects and persists into the future over time and, although subject to development, is essentially always identifiable as being the same, in terms of being socioculturally agreed. Often characteristics of national identity are framed in this way in popular culture, as are individuals in the way they are labelled. On the other hand, there is the more fluid notion of identities or even subjectivities which are not essentialist but emerge from situation to situation according to how we position ourselves or are positioned in different discursive settings. This latter view of identities and subjectivities is viewed as post-structural or sometimes referred to as post-modern in art and literature because they are not viewed as being held in place by any inner linguistic or discursive structure. They are indeed the ingredients of intersubjectivity since the individual cannot be isolated from them within an illusory sameness or 'idem'. We will see in the next chapter, that for Derrida, there is only the signifier, rather than the signified, and this transmits an ungrounded identity, where language identity is viewed post-structurally as fluid without any grounding within structure, either psychological, social or linguistic.

For Ricoeur, signs are experienced by individuals within the narratives they construct and so what is important for individuals is the story they tell themselves, and others over time. Ricoeur holds to a more stable form of identity which can be formed into a narrative predicated on the notion of time. Jansen (2015) outlines Ricoeur's notion that 'time is configured as a narrative'. Time is then structured as narrative since people conceptualize time in terms of the events that they have experienced over time. Time is then a mental construction through narrative rather than any absolute conceptualization, beyond our perception. The past is then, for us, how we give account of the events and signs that we have experienced, and the narrative of this in speech and writing is a way of making disparate events and signs cohere into a life story or part of a life story that can constitute our identity. In a sense we use signs for our narrative rather than deconstructing them to see how they are composed. For a patriot the flag in its totality such as the Tricolore or the Union Flag is important in how it contributes to his/her narrative rather than the meaning of the constituent parts unless of course one of the constituent parts is to be used for another national narrative. If, for example, for Scottish nationalists the Scottish cross or the Saltire is important for a present and future narrative of independence, the sign that will carry the narrative is the external sign of the Saltire rather than St Andrew. Many who regard this white cross on a blue background as especially significant for the mission of independence will see it as such because it corresponds to their narrative rather than because of its more interior association with a Christian saint. This, I believe, reinforces the dual nature of the sign in having both a more interior purpose and an external communicative purpose. Much more will be said about signs and semiotics in Chapter 9.

Therefore, time past and present going into the future, as in the example above of a mission for independence, is narrative and as such it is text, spoken, written or semiotic in the form of image or gesture. This narrative can be ultimately internalized in a Vygostskian sense so that it becomes part of our inner voice and ultimately psychology. Ricoeur's approach is that this forms a part of a unitary life story where everything is pieced together.

Almon (2017) however questions the notion of a single unitary and continuous life story of the self. Almon quotes Foucault's statement that 'subjectivity is constituted by the internalization of a host of social and historic factors that determine how people think, live and speak' (2017; p183). This self is then not an essentialist self but constructed in a variety of life situations with other people's voices, creating a variety of selves which are again intersubjectivities. Ricoeur, however, would argue that it is within the agency of the individual to create a metadiscourse to attempt to make these selves cohere into an overarching narrative. Crowley (2003) indeed states that Freud in his clinical work helped patients to make sense of chaotic or incoherent lives by constructing meaningful life stories, so providing a sense of order.

Again, we encounter the debate between the free will of the individual versus determinism. If a narrative for a coherent identity is drawn from text, the consequence of what we experience within the disparate intersubjective texts that we traverse becomes normalized, in a deliberate act of free will, into a unitary metanarrative. However, a metatext that we might set up to construct coherence may simply be seen as just another narrative text amongst others as opposed to a privileged unitary discourse. Texts, seen in this way, can then exist horizontally side by side without any hierarchy of overriding importance. This means that lives are no more than a variety of different texts and the narrative is just another text. This relativism of course presents a danger of a lack of grounding of which Ricoeur was well aware, and consequently a lack of direction. Individual free will suggests however that individuals do have the agency to establish a critical discourse of analysis to establish coherence, but such agency is always a matter of debate because one could argue that it is not unitary since, as Bakhtin suggests, it will always contain the voices of others or speak from a particular position. The concept of metadiscourse and metalinguistic analysis is explored in the Conclusion.

We have to be careful in this debate that we do not engage in intellectual inconsistency in saying that people's consciousness becomes subject to dispersal in all the disparate discourses in which they become immersed and yet it is only the philosopher who can bring all this together into a critical discursive meta-analysis and thereby adopt for her/himself a Godlike position overseeing all this multiplicity. There is either the possibility of a meta-analytical discourse or there is not and since it seems that there is such a philosophical discourse encompassing and researching multiple discursive identities, people themselves generally can engage in critical discursive analysis in secondary, higher or continuing education to become more linguistically self-aware. This should not then be just the preserve of academic philosophers but an integral part of secondary and higher education, transcending the narrative towards a more critically analytic language and discourse.

Without this critical analysis there is a danger that, in real-life situations, individuals who, unquestioningly, engage in fantasy narratives in online virtual reality may, it is mooted, have difficulty separating fantasy from fiction. Within the fantasy they align themselves to the powerful voices and images of others. It is often argued that this can lead to violent behaviour and in the case of extreme pornography, violent sexual behaviour and in the case of online racial or religious propaganda, radicalization in extreme politics and religion. Others argue that this is not the case, that individuals retain sufficient agency to follow moral courses of action in the real world despite their experiences of the virtual world. This is an ongoing debate, but Ricoeur suggests that it is only ethical action that will guarantee agency in constructing a stable narrative identity.

Ethical action

Crowley (2003) states that 'Ricoeur seeks to stabilize signification and save the identity of the subject by appealing to a greater good beyond narrative identity, namely a coherent notion of self-identity that ethically responds to the call of the other' (2003; p6). I argue here that, recalling Bakhtin, we are socially interactive beings, and our linguistic utterances and texts cannot exist on their own. They need a reader or listener who can be seen as the Other in our interactions. This is the interactive and intersubjective context where textual meaning-making and interpretation are worked out since anticipating the response of the other and then understanding how others see us can become a moral guide to how we are and how we see ourselves. So, we can only be ethical beings in social interaction through spoken and written texts enacted intersubjectively as linguistic behaviour and ethical action towards others. Crowley states, 'Thus Ricoeur defers the defining moments to the world of ethical action. It is the world of praxis, he argues, that finally stabilizes meaning' (2003; p8). According to Ricoeur, the stability of narrative identity finally exists by linking language to action in the fulfilment of a promise. It is this concept of the promise in terms of ethics that renders language performative in keeping one's word with regard to the other. Of course, performative language is of itself, by definition, linguistic behaviour where language and action are so closely connected that the former can be seen as causal. Crowley (2003) concludes by that, the answer to the question 'Who am I?' resides in one's response to the other because, 'Ultimately moral action defines personal identity and subsumes narrative identity within the greater cause of ethical order' (2003; p8).

My argument is that the link between narrative and ethical action also needs an intervening element of a critically analytical language which can survey narrative language and I argue for such a language in Chapter 9 and the Conclusion.

The linguistic 'other' in foreign language education as ethical action

Here I argue that our narrative identity is relational and contains the 'Other' within a Bakhtinian intersubjectivity which is a continuous dialectical interrelation between how we see others and how others see us and addresses the cultural other or 'alterity' in ethics. In a local sense, another person alone is a cultural otherness coming from a different group culture in a different community or perhaps the same community but from different families, different age groups, social classes and genders. If we then go to a different country, we encounter similar categorical cultural differences in alterity although within the cultural framework of another country, due to its language, educational system, sociopolitical and economic system, etc. It seems then that narrative identity does contain alterity in one's relationship with others and this has to be necessarily the case because we inhabit the world with others. Alterity in general comes to us through social interaction including the digital world of media platforms and of course we can interact with others daily on social media even if we live alone. This interaction has an ethical substance in the content of our interaction in terms of how we want to be perceived and, in such media interaction, Ricoeur's notion of ethical narrative is particularly relevant in its capacity to constitute individuals as morally good or not so good.

In foreign language education, as an example of ethical behaviour, our view of alterity is particularly salient because interrelationships with those who are other than ourselves as a community are seen as intercultural or cross-cultural (Kramsch 1998) and, seek 'ways to understand the Other on the other side of the border by learning his/her language' (1998; p81).

I argue that foreign language education is an area particularly highlighting the border line between ourselves and alterity and our approach to language learning in this context, whether technically we are good at it or not, shows us something of ourselves.

Evans (2018) highlights the concept of 'Languaculture' proposed by Van Lier where, 'a new language contains new and different realities which amount to new ways of seeing the world and new possibilities for the learner's exploration of self and identity' (2018; p224).

If we consider secondary school research that I undertook for my previous book, 'Language, Identity and Symbolic Culture' (Evans 2018) which took place in a comprehensive community school in the south of England which I can now fictionalize as Sandhill Academy, we see, below, two students interviewed regarding their approach to alterity in language and culture. They too are anonymized as Jade, a female student and Richard, a male student in year 11, aged sixteen years and approaching GCSE exams. Below are brief dialogues between me as researcher (DE) showing the extent these two students are interested in the culture of the other.

Excerpt from interview with Jade.

Jade – J; Researcher – DE.

DE- Do you think it is important to understand the way other people live in different countries?

J- Yeh, it's different cultures and knowing how other people live apart from British people and ourselves, so yeh it's good.

DE- Why is it good d'you think?

J- Again with language and everything, learning a different language, you get to meet new people and know how other people live their lives and what cultures people have.

DE- Ok, fine. Do you think – so would you say you are interested in the life and culture of other countries?

J- Yeh, definitely because it's interesting to know how other people live apart from yourself.

It seems from this dialogue that Jade has an identity narrative of alterity, encompassing cultural difference to explore her own identity. The idea therefore of the other in narrative identity is that it can be integrated to one's own sense of self to enhance one's own identity rather than constrain it behind a boundary of sameness.

Excerpt from interview with Richard.

R – Richard; Researcher – DE.

DE- What about you Richard, do you have a feeling for the sound of the language? (referring to French).

R- Yeh, I think it's important that they've got the accent but we have our accent. It's one thing having a different language but it's very unique and I think that's great. I like it.

DE- Would you like to get to know French people well?

R- yeh, pen friends or something. That would really help. I think they should do that more often, because you would be socializing and you'd be growing on their ideas.

Here we see part of another young student's identity narrative which encompasses both language and culture. Richard wants to explore different ideas for his own development.

We can see then examples of narrative identity which is ethical in its positive regard for alterity. Narrative identity can be an expansion of self, projecting itself towards the future wherein the two interviewees have an implicit regard for the future in terms of how positive it would be to explore language-culture going forward. The narrative identity consequently is intersubjective in that it contains the notion of the alterity of different cultures.

Nevertheless, there are post-structural arguments against what could be seen as a colonizing view of narrative identity in that it could be seen as colonizing alterity by incorporating it into one's expanding sense of self. This is then seen as denying otherness. It is consequently important to emphasize that the encounter of two language-cultures is not the encounter of two monoliths of different samenesses where one may colonize the other in an expansion of identity. It is rather an encounter of difference since within each apparent sameness in the encounter is a series of differences in such as social class, gender, ethnicity and language dialects amongst other differences. We will explore the post-structural view of alterity in the next chapter where identity is viewed as fluid and multiple and not viewed from any central holding position, within language and discourse.

The following interview is with a female student in the younger age group of year nine and therefore fourteen years of age. The student is called Georgina (a fictionalized name for the sake of anonymity in the same school). The interview focuses on Georgina's studies in Spanish. This interview shows an appreciation of the alterity of cultural identity within the foreign language.

The dialogue is between DE (myself as researcher) and G – Georgina.

DE- D'you think that language and culture go together?

G- yeh, coz your language kind of reflects your culture like some people use slang.

DE- yeh.

G- and that reflects the way they are and are brought up.

DE- So do you think the more you get to know the culture the better you learn the language?

G- yeh coz the more you learn the culture, like you were teaching us about Castilian that Spanish culture is reflected in their Castilian Spanish and the South American non-Castilian Spanish reflects culture.

Georgina understands that the alterity or the otherness in culture resides inside the language and seems to be able to appreciate difference in identity and the way it is expressed in the foreign language of Castilian and South American Spanish.

I have chosen foreign language education as an area of narrative identity development which goes beyond the mechanical learning of a language. It concerns learning the culture of difference around the language and just as importantly the culture of difference within the language. This is because, as we have seen in Part Two of this book, grammatical structure and lexis contain a culture of difference in the way they are constructed so that a foreign language is not a word-for-word translation of one's own native language. French for example is not English in translation but instead offers up a way of seeing the world which is slightly different because of the way in which it maps itself onto reality is slightly different from English or another language.

I would also argue that it is not just foreign language education that offers an opportunity for exploration of narrative identity. In general, the Humanities provide interpretation and exploration of identity narrative with regard to alterity in such subjects as English literature, History, Human Geography, Social Sciences and Drama.

I argue however that foreign language education is particularly relevant to narrative identity formation because it is concerned with the crossing of cultural borders and with future possibilities for identity development since the learning of language and culture is a long-term process going forward into the future. Dornyei and Ushioda (2009) maintain that identity contains an element of the future within it, so that when one incorporates an activity within one's narrative identity, one may well envision how one's identity will be, carrying that activity forward into the future. Nevertheless, this idea of future identity linked to current activity relates also to such activities as sports, artistic or musical activity and this is also linked to the notion of the other in terms of how one will be perceived by others and how these perceptions will feed back into one's own identity.

Therefore, existentially, one exists to some degree through the eyes of others and furthermore, existentially, one's regard is to the future in terms of how one's identity will be in their eyes and consequently in one's own eyes at a future time.

The future as an alterity

In Ricoeur's view narrative identity exists on a time border as a frontier with alterity as well as an alterity with the 'Other' as individuals. These border lands are construed by Homi Bhabba (1994) as 'third places'. The 'third place' is an area of identity formation where one has left one's original place in culture and time and yet one is in transit, not having arrived at destination. Narrative identity is then not completed but a hybrid between a former identity and a future identity based on Ricoeur's notion of time as narrative. This hybridity becomes an identity in itself, always in motion towards a new place. In this sense identity is always unfinished and in the process of 'becoming' rather than 'being'.

The notion of identity as becoming, so that where we are is always in some sort of transit, suggests a fluid identity, a sort of 'never-ending story'. Narrative identity where the past and the future, conceptualized in the present, are made to cohere is somewhat packaged for ready understanding, rather like a professional CV. The unitary narrative identity provides a security and a grounding which may be illusory because it leaves out in the margins many aspects that refuse coherence.

Sheerin (2009) expresses beautifully this dispersal of the forgotten constituents of identity in the following observation:

> We noted how our past is populated by former selves – infant, child, adolescent, young adult. These act like national identities that reduce contemporary and past difference to the identical. But if we prise open these high-level categories we will be surprised by the manifold that is hidden beneath: the me that started school, that first walked, the me in the photograph on the beach, the me that mother told me spoke its first word, the me that first loved, the bespectacled, the athletic, the obdurate, the coy, the crazy, the abstract, the animal, the idiotic me. And such selves can be re-formulated and re-negotiated just like national identities. There is no end to the multiplicity of little selves that have inhabited these personal nations, each of which has lived a little life, sparkled briefly and had its light extinguished. (2009; p166)

The insightful statement of Sheerin is that these mini-identities are very much like Bakhtin's heteroglossia inside the unitary narrative identity that we have constructed for the coherence of our life, for our ready understanding for us and others like a CV or LinkedIn profile page. This does not deny the validity of Ricoeur's notion of narrative identity and does not say that it is some kind of fabrication. Far from it, narrative identity is our enactment of agency in a world that, without our mechanism of a centre of gravity, would appear incoherent and without meaning. Our weaving together a narrative from the disparate experiences that we traverse is not a fiction, but it is a framing of events to constitute sameness of identity and exclude difference towards the margins. However, as such, argues Sheerin (2009) it does not represent all we are because we have left a great deal out of our CV which might be items that do not conveniently fit in or even that cause us shame if we were to include them. Narrative identity tells a truth, an acceptable morally righteous truth for the occasion, but not the whole truth. It works like language because, like standard language and grammar, narrative identity holds together at the centre for coherence whereas at the margins, language disperses into dialects and slang. So, in a sense, a single unitary notion of identity, as an analogy, albeit extreme, would be the futile attempt at trying to catch the river with our bare hands. Consequently, we need to talk about identities as differences as well as sameness, and also the fluidity of these identities because, to retain the analogy of the flowing water of the river, the identities are ongoing and flowing through time.

Conclusion

Sheerin observes, 'For there are important "remainders" that cannot be accounted for by the theory of self as narrative' (2009; p169) and in the next chapter, we will explore language and identity as difference rather than sameness; identity brought in from the margins, identities as streams of consciousness occasioned by language use and deconstruction, where deconstruction means bringing forgotten and marginalized identities to the surface to disrupt hegemony of rigid narratives. We will explore how power has banished these meanings to the edges of life in the sameness of a hegemony of meaning to which we are all encouraged to subscribe by popular media, so that being unaware of powerful heteroglossia, many people all say the same thing using the same cultural references and thereby risk adopting similar media-constructed narrative identities. In doing this, I do not discard narrative identity, which is useful for its coherence, but I argue that narrative identity misses the full picture in terms of the qualitative messiness of identities as we pass through time.

Ricoeur's notion of narrative identity has its place and usefulness in what might seem a troubled, incoherent world but this is much like a CV or, as we have already mentioned a profile page on LinkedIn. These identity tools are necessary, but they discard much and suppress much about an individual. Ricoeur does acknowledge the 'ipseity' of selfhood within identity but this future 'other' is yet still only a possibility, in a 'ghostly' existence without the ontology of substance that sameness possesses.

There is then an openness to the future concealed within narrative identity because it is always populated by alterity albeit suppressed and as we will see, the sameness in identity breaks up in 'deconstruction'. The two alterities which are at the edge of sameness and within sameness are the alterities of the future and the 'other'.

We have nonetheless stated that narrative identity is a feature of an individual's agency in creating a story and yet at the same time we have to ask what story and for whose consumption and for what purpose? The narrative identity that is constructed may well be, unknowingly shaped by powerful discourses if we have little critical awareness that narratives are indeed frequently constructed from the voices of others.

The next chapter looks more closely at the differences that make up identities rather than the sameness.

Part Four

Beyond Structure

8

Phenomenology and Post Structuralism in Language

Introduction

In this chapter I argue that language and identity are multiple and multilayered, as a consequence of difference.

Building on the rationally mind-based grammatical identity of Part One, we have seen that language has to hold together at the centre to be intelligible internally before becoming externally facing as social communication. The Chomskyan sentence, 'Colorless dreams sleep furiously' has a grammatical identity but no social identity. It may have a poetical identity and it makes a grammatical sense even if not a socially functional sense. For statements to make sense socially, they have to have a social identity in that they have to be socially shaped. So, the noun, verb and adjective/adverb have to have a social resonance which is a semantic rationality as opposed to just a grammatical rationality. Therefore, a sentence such as 'I sleep peacefully' would be socially understood.

We saw the last chapter on narrative identity evoking two basic layers of identity. Firstly, the narrative identity of sameness within its spoken or written text having an internally intelligible identity at its core with a surrounding narrative to contain a coherent story. If we say that a narrative identity is a reordering of disparate experiences into a coherent story, having a social identity, this means it is socially shaped or even socially determined. The coherence is based on maximizing sameness and suppressing incoherent differences in order to correspond to salient social realities. Sameness, in order to maintain conventional social understanding as in a CV or social media profile, is held in place by discursive social power shaped by social interaction. This means that identities may come to be excluded or marginalized if they do not correspond with a socially recognizable narrative.

Secondly Ricoeur speaks of the identity of difference in the self-hood of ipse as opposed to the sameness of idem. Narrative identity contains difference, this may be suppressed difference, but it is the 'spectre' of becoming, the encounter with the possibilities of the future and the encounter with the alterity of others. These are the two alterities that we 'spoke' about in the last chapter: the alterity of the future and the alterity of the 'Other'. Sameness therefore has a hidden encounter with alterity in these two fronts, the encounter with the future and the encounter with others which are two fronts of alterity. This statement will lead us to 'deconstruction' later in the chapter to answer the question of where are these alterities of difference to be found in and around apparent sameness?

Without discarding the narrative identity, we need now to move to a more phenomenological approach to identity in terms of difference rather than sameness. This means focusing on the notion of multiple identities of difference shaped by different language types and discourses which might fall outside of a coherent narrative or be suppressed within it. This approach paints a fuller picture of identity in both its sameness and its difference.

The theoretical standpoint I will adopt for a more multiple view of identity is based on the work of the phenomenologist philosopher Henri Bergson.

Bergson

Much of what Bergson outlines can be summed up at the beginning of his seminal work, *Creative Evolution*, when he states, 'I change then without ceasing' (1998; p1). He further states on the very first page of 'Creative Evolution', '...there is no feeling, no volition which is not undergoing change every moment; if a mental state ceased to vary, its duration would cease to flow' (1998).

In this way Bergson 'sets out his stall' very early on in terms of the notion of a flow of subjectivity. Much in the same way as Ricoeur, time plays an important part due to the notion of time as duration. So, this is not measured time in minutes, hours and days, etc. but the idea of the past flowing forward into the present and then the present into a 'yet to be' future as a continuous indistinct flux where, no sooner that the present is here, than it is already gone. So, we change because our past moments are continually merging from past to present, forming fluid identities. Bergson asserts then, 'We are creating ourselves continually' (1998; p7). 'Inner life then exists in a disparate flow and eludes our intellect. Time is then, only as we experience it. We don't know if, indeed, there is such a thing as time outside our perception of it.'

It is important to note that Ricoeur's narrative identity is backward facing and not in a constant flux. Here narrative identity is constructed in retrospect whereas Bergsonian identity is concerned with subjectivities in the moment which are unanalysed lived experiences. It is only later through reflective language that these lived experiences are ordered into a backward looking narrative. At the moment of live experience Bergson argues that the flow of life as it is felt at the moment of experience overflows and eludes the intellect. So, the flow of life moves forward into the present whereas narrative identity looks backwards to the past. However, this is not to dispel or discard narrative identity, it is rather to interrogate its truth. Narrative identity may be functional and therefore necessary in focusing on the sameness which addresses a particular role in life rather than a truthful difference that does not cohere for the purpose of that role. This is a question of discourse, so a CV would be a professional discourse and might not include aspects of identity such as 'heavy metal' or 'acid house' music and culture or Tibetan Buddhism spirituality. These important aspects of lived experience would be left off unless an employer interested in the whole person asks a candidate if s/he has any special interests or hobbies. Even then one might leave off the above and include more conventional activities such as sea fishing or sailing. These are rather frivolous examples, but they do show how narrative identity is likely to be shaped by the power of a dominant discourse and thereby sidelined, to the margins, that which is deemed irrelevant or inappropriate. This is part of the answer to the question above as to where difference lies in and around sameness in narrative. A dominant discourse excludes it in the margins.

Therefore, Bergson differentiates between life lived existentially and life rationalized retrospectively in the following way, 'Of course, when once the road has been travelled, we can glance over it, mark its direction, note this in psychological terms and speak of it as if there had been the pursuit of an end' (1998; p51). The discourse of reflection is then a strategically constructed one and different from existentially lived experience since for Bergson the road is created in the act of travelling over it. I think by this metaphor we are able to understand that there is a phenomenological subjectivity created in the act of being and speaking spontaneous language and then afterwards a construction of more stable narrative identity through a metalanguage of reflection.

We might consider the following extract from Virginia Woolf's novel *The Waves* as an example of the Bergsonian notion of the flow of life which also illustrates Peirce's notion of 'firstness' (Atkin 2016; p297):

The text below taken from *The Waves* by Virginia Woolf (1931) illustrates the 'firstness' of experiences where the characters Bernard, Neville, Jinny and

Susan experience a slice of life as it happens. We do not know the context and in the extract, there is no analysis and so there is only a 'firstness' of life.

> Up here Bernard, Neville, Jinny and Susan (but not Rhoda) skim the flower-beds with their nets. They skim the butterflies from the nodding tops of the flowers. They brush the surface of the world. Their nets are full of fluttering wings. "Louis! Louis! Louis!" they shout. But they cannot see me. I am on the other side of the hedge. There are only little eyeholes among the leaves. Oh Lord, let them pass. Lord, let them lay their butterflies on a pocket-handkerchief on the gravel. Let them count out their tortoiseshells, their red admirals and cabbage whites. But let me be unseen. I am green as a yew tree in the shade of the hedge. My hair is made of leaves. I am rooted to the middle of the earth. My body is a stalk. I press the stalk. A drop oozes from the hole at the mouth and slowly, thickly, grows larger and larger. Now something pink passes the eyehole. Now an eye-beam is slid through the chink. Its beam strikes me. I am a boy in a grey flannel suit. She has found me. I am struck on the nape of the neck. She has kissed me. All is shattered.

This seems like a game of hide and seek from Louis' point of view in that he is hiding from the others whether or not they are actively seeking him. Louis is hoping not to be caught and trying to merge in with the undergrowth, hugging the ground with leaves on his head. Louis is commenting this action and Woolf uses the present tense so that the reader experiences what Louis is experiencing. With regard to identity we, the reader, might feel that this is an unfinished subjectivity since we do not know how this will end nor Louis' relationship with his peers.

> 'I was running,' said Jinny, after breakfast.
>
> I saw leaves moving in a hole in the hedge. I thought "That is a bird on its nest." I parted them and looked; but there was no bird on a nest. The leaves went on moving. I was frightened. I ran past Susan, past Rhoda, and Neville and Bernard in the tool-house talking. I cried as I ran, faster and faster. What moved the leaves? What moves my heart, my legs? And I dashed in here, seeing you green as a bush, like a branch, very still, Louis, with your eyes fixed. "Is he dead?" I thought, and kissed you, with my heart jumping under my pink frock like the leaves, which go on moving, though there is nothing to move them. Now I smell geraniums; I smell earth mould. I dance. I ripple. I am thrown over you like a net of light. I lie quivering flung over you.

Here we see the same scene, as above from Jinny's point of view on the other side of the edge where she sees Louis from the same hole as in the first extract. Jinny finishes by sprawling all over Louis and kissing him on his neck. Again, the present tense is used in what is usually referred to as Woolf's stream of consciousness style of writing, capturing the quick of life.

'Through the chink in the hedge,' said Susan,

> I saw her kiss him. I raised my head from my flower-pot and looked through a chink in the hedge. I saw her kiss him. I saw them, Jinny and Louis, kissing. Now I will wrap my agony inside my pocket-handkerchief. It shall be screwed tight into a ball. I will go to the beech wood alone, before lessons. I will not sit at a table, doing sums. I will not sit next Jinny and next Louis. I will take my anguish and lay it upon the roots under the beech trees. I will examine it and take it between my fingers. They will not find me. I shall eat nuts and peer for eggs through the brambles and my hair will be matted and I shall sleep under hedges and drink water from ditches and die there.

The events are moving on from one person to another. The scenery stays the same, with the same hole in the hedge but the dynamic of the events changes and this time we see the psychological reality of Susan who has witnessed the event of Jinny kissing Louis. We see her distraught psychological state and how she copes with it, and so we seamlessly, as readers, experience a flow of reality as we move from person to person and physical to psychological reality all within the same event.

'Susan has passed us,' said Bernard. 'She has passed the tool-house door with her handkerchief screwed into a ball. She was not crying, but her eyes, which are so beautiful, were narrow as cats' eyes before they spring. I shall follow her, Neville. I shall go gently behind her, to be at hand, with my curiosity, to comfort her when she bursts out in a rage and thinks, "I am alone."

We move on to Bernard's reaction now as he sees the outward appearance of Susan's psychological state and his desire to comfort her in her distress.

> Now she walks across the field with a swing, nonchalantly, to deceive us. Then she comes to the dip; she thinks she is unseen; she begins to run with her fists clenched in front of her. Her nails meet in the ball of her pocket-handkerchief. She is making for the beech woods out of the light. She spreads her arms as she comes to them and takes to the shade like a swimmer. But she is blind after the light and trips and flings herself down on the roots under the trees, where the light seems to pant in and out, in and out. The branches heave up and down. There is agitation and trouble here. There is gloom. The light is fitful. There is anguish here. The roots make a skeleton on the ground, with dead leaves heaped in the angles. Susan has spread her anguish out. Her pocket-handkerchief is laid on the roots of the beech trees and she sobs, sitting crumpled where she has fallen.
> (*The Waves* by Virginia Woolf; pp7–9, Penguin Classics 2019)

Finally, the action, both physical and psychological, moves back to Susan as we see her go into hiding and collapse under the trees.

The interesting and insightful nature of this text is that, as the reader, we experience first-hand how a physical event can impact psychology where Jinny kissing Louis results in Susan's emotional collapse and Bernard's desire to comfort. There is no writer analysis or thirdness; instead this is left to the reader to experience life as the characters experience it. Identity is in the action, events and subjective experience, framed phenomenologically as subjectivity constructed in the moment.

This is far from a narrative coherent objective identity, based on common elements from the social world to construct an intersubjectivity of understanding. The reality presented here is analogous to how we might experience day-to-day life or events in our life which no one else can really understand; so, no one can understand the joy or anguish or heartache exactly as 'you' experience it. Woolf, in her text, attempts to enter or really construct the mind of Susan so that we can experience her heartache and even though we will never experience life in exactly the same way as she does, there is enough material for our empathy. Consequently, we can to some extent imagine how jealousy or heartache must feel for Susan, probably because, being human and given to similar life experiences as other humans, we may already have a psychological potentiality for jealousy and/or heartache within us.

The construction of the phenomenological identity

Crowley (2003) describes 'three successive moments' of Ricoeur's notion of narrative identity (2003; p2). There is the first moment which is live in the world experience as it happens, an 'experience of being-in-the world' (2003; p2). This 'illustrates' the 'elan vital' of life as it is happening right now. My use of the word 'illustrates' is ambiguous because this suggests that it narrates or shows an event that has in effect happened from the writer's or speaker's point of view and yet the idea of first moment in Woolf's 'stream of consciousness' writing is that the event is actually happening in the writing or in the spoken commentary. This might of course be problematic because the event surely must come first, at least in the mind of the writer, in order for it to be illustrated. However, as we will see below Virginia Woolf uses the present tense so that the reader experiences the event as it is occurring. The extract above shows the flow of life and yet how narrow the gap is between Woolf's thought and its representation in writing is debatable. A possible view is that the gap between conscious thought and writing is extremely narrow to enable this sense of immediate quick of life presence. A more radical view is that the consciousness is actually inside the text at the moment of writing or indeed speaking, as though the thought and the pen were as one.

The second stage or 'second moment' is putting the action into the context of a narrative plot which supports and makes sense of the action and the third stage or 'third moment' is the analysis of what the narrative scene signifies leading to 'a transformative understanding of oneself in the world' (2003; p3). These three successive moments from the sense of being-in-the-world subjectivity through to the final narrative identity of understanding one's position in the world are very reminiscent of Peirce's notion of 'firstness', 'secondness' and 'thirdness' (Atkin 2016; pp297–300) which we will encounter more fully in Chapter 9 on signs and semiotics in identity formation.

In the example of 'first moment' taken from the extract above, we witness the flow or overflowing of life within written language before any analysis has taken place. Bergson, although not a linguist, alludes to the power of language, by stating that without language, human intelligence would have been limited to the perception of natural material objects. The production of material objects as sociocultural products which requires linguistic social interaction would never have occurred. He argues that it is due to the transferability of the word, from meaning to meaning, that has allowed human focus to shift from the material to the reflective. Bergson states, 'Now this mobility of words, that makes them able to pass from one thing to another, has enabled them to be extended from things to ideas' (1998; p158). Recalling Saussure's separation of the signified from the signifier in Chapter 4, we see that the word is mobile and free enough to join with other words to form a reflective discourse, detached from material experiences and objects. This mobility of the word accounts for its interpretive nature, given that a word can attract many meanings and so the flow of words means that interpretive closure is impossible. Text, in terms of interpretation, consequently, remains open.

Ansell-Pearson (2018) argues that Bergson attempts to transcend the limits of the human condition imposed by traditional philosophers such as Kant, by proposing intuitive knowledge – which is knowledge of lived experience in the moment. Kant contended that we cannot know the world beyond perception and in more modern times Wittgenstein proposed that the limits of language are the limits of knowledge. Bergson however contends that subjectively we know life as we live it and then after the event, we put it into words, but life always overflows and exceeds language. So, we know life by our intuition according to Bergson and this rejects the intellectualization of knowledge. Furthermore, he contends in his work 'Creative Evolution' that life recreates itself and transferred to social life, we, as individuals, recreate ourselves in multiple subjectivities in multiple discourses moment by moment. We have already seen in the work of Bakhtin that our flow of text and speech is interpenetrated by the voices of others and the consequence of this is that our identities are not unitary but partly constituted by the voices of others. This has interesting ramifications for multilingualism and multiculturalism shaped by the Bakhtinian centrifugal nature of language-culture in its movement towards difference. Ansell-Pearson (2018) in his work on Bergson quotes him as saying that 'We must resist the temptation to place on hold nature with our own ideas or shrink reality to the measure of them. We should not allow our need for a unity of knowledge to impose itself upon the multiplicity of nature (2018; p14). He furthermore quotes, '… the mind cannot be restricted to the intellect since it overflows it' (2018; p13).

Applied to language and identity, the consequences of ready-made categories of identity through language is the suppression of differences in identity through an artificial enforcement of sameness. My argument here is then for a questioning of ready-made identities occasioned through language by exploring the differences that may be contained within an imposed sameness. This, then, is the second part of the answer to the question above, of finding difference within sameness, which involves unpicking the word categories of sameness to reveal the differences within the category. In education an example of this might be a reluctant student of modern languages saying, 'Why should I speak French because I'm English?'. But what does English mean as an identity category regarding language use? Given that most people throughout the non-English-speaking world are bilingual or even multilingual, monolingualism appears to be a culturally imposed sameness occurring through speaking a dominant language. So English monolingualism is prevalent because it is a dominant sociopolitical category which marginalizes other languages, including community heritage languages. There are, however, educational and pedagogical benefits, in terms of widening identities and perspectives, from exploring difference in language and culture. Unfortunately, conversely, there are regretfully examples of minority languages being suppressed by more economically dominant languages in an attempt to propagate a language-culture hegemony. This can be seen in the Uyghur province of north-west China where Uyghur language and culture are being repressed by the economically powerful mainstream Chinese Han language and culture (Evans 2014).

The reverse side of Bergson's phenomenological philosophy, when applied to language and sign as Derrida does in the next section, seems to be the absence of interiority, in a rejection of essentialism. We will see how Derrida takes this to the level where there are no such things as a signified and where everything becomes forward-flowing signs. This leaves no room for interior meaning beyond intersubjective agreement and so nature loses its ability to contain signs because everything is humanly constructed. We will discuss the interiority/exteriority dichotomy in signs later in the book. Fixed categories, therefore, for Bergson, are only a starting point for identity and not a finality or essentialist endpoint where identity can rest. Nevertheless, there can be intersubjective agreement in terms of a convention for identity and this is witnessed in daily life in clubs and institutions or even countries where there are mission statements and constitutions. These texts could be deconstructed in textual analysis yet there may be intersubjective agreement, through the power arrangements that obtain, that certain conventions will bear the identity of a particular organization. After all Saussure had stated that word meanings, once they had lost their word-object one to one signification, only existed by conventional association.

An example of a dominant conventionally agreed identity in text is in the following newspaper headline in the Daily Express of Wednesday 19 September 2018 which states:

'Brexit Plan Delivers Freedoms People Voted For'

However, there could be a political debate about what these freedoms are exactly several years on from the referendum vote in 2016 and although such political debate is beyond the remit of this book, 'Freedoms' is a word label which needs to be examined. What are the 'freedoms' and who benefits from them are the questions that need to be asked in order to fully understand the word label. Also, in terms of answering the question posed earlier in the chapter with regard to finding difference within sameness, we can ask who exactly does the term 'People' refer to? The conventional meaning that the headline writer is constructing in addressing her/his conceptualization of the likely reader is everyone, as in 'The People' as a unit of sameness. However, in a linguistic sense, 'People' might mean, not 'The People' but merely 'Some People' because lots of other people voted against Brexit and these voters lost by a very small percentage of the popular vote. Therefore, in deconstructing the word, 'People' we can arrive at another meaning of difference as a true statement. It is possible then that this headline of 'People' could be interpreted both ways either 'The People' or 'Some People'. It would seem then that conventional understanding as part of an easy ready-made identity can be unpackaged to reveal the difference rather than an illusory sameness.

A word bearing multiple meanings is known as polysemia, and amongst possible meanings, it is often just the most conventionally agreed meaning that prevails. Derrida (1997, 1978) would see this outcome as a function of power where alternative meanings have been suppressed and marginalized. Derrida holds that identities are constituted by difference but held in sameness by power. In the next section, we will focus on Derrida and how his deconstruction project is a celebration of difference in identity.

Derrida and deconstruction

Derrida follows Bergson in his criticism of traditional philosophy, and, in the case of Derrida, this criticism is focused on the illusory notion of Presence. Traditional Western philosophy going as far back as Plato has based its statements and, by extension ideas of identity as sameness, on the notion of presence which for Derrida is illusory. Presence for Derrida is a result of the power of conventionality based on repetition. We can see that 'sacrosanct' identities are often celebrated in ritual such as religious services or state events adorned by marching bands and military parades. Such events give an illusion of hyper-presence and, much else which is not in focus is pushed to the margins. The project of deconstruction justifies the margins, elevating them to the level of front and centre due to the fact that, stripped of the power of presence, they are all constituted equally in text. Textual analysis in deconstruction subverts normative common sense views of meanings held in place through power.

Bush (2009) states about Derrida, 'Derrida articulates his position that "nothing is outside the text (il n'y a pas de hors-texte), challenging every philosophical attempt to ground knowledge and linguistic meaning by appeal to some sort of foundation, principle, or entity independent of human history and culture"' (Bush 2009; p45). The key thing to note is that for Derrida everything is text – signs, words, speech, images, etc. and these things are signifiers without any ground – they exist and move forward in time through text. Presence through the power of speech and then subsequent writing, to provide a sense of permanence, is illusory. There is then no such thing as pure presence. Presence tries to form itself, but it is always, as an identity, unfinished. This is because signs move on through time and are always open to interpretation and reinterpretation as time goes by. Derrida refers to this as deferral where, from the moment one speaks and is heard or writes and is read, one loses control of the message because the message or the text travels into the future, especially with modern media, and one can no longer control how it will be interpreted. So, there is no presence that sits there like a static identity unless it is upheld in power. One does not have on the one hand identities and then on the other hand, language which represents these identities. All one has is language and identities that are constituted in this language and more generally in text.

Derrida is able to deconstruct presence through time and difference or in his own terms deferral and difference from which he coins the neologism 'la différance' (spelt with an 'a') to combine both terms. He contends that because of the separation of signified from signifier there cannot be finality in interpretations and words themselves, which, as we have already mentioned, take on different meanings over time and place. This slippage in meaning can be seen as an immediate example between the English word 'Cult' and the French word 'Un Culte' where in the former it designates marginalized and sometimes clandestine spirituality or culture often centred around a charismatic leader and in the latter, mainstream organized spirituality mainly in the form of Christian worship. Both variations have the same commonality at their root but have developed different specific meanings over time. The word may continue to develop more cultural and non-religious meanings over time such as 'cult movie' or 'cult book' having more to do with fashion than religion in a more secular society as social context also evolves. Another example of meaning slippage between English and French is the word 'Escapade' spelt exactly the same in both languages. In French 'Une Escapade' is an escape in the sense of the tourism notion of 'getting away from it all' whereas, as it has crossed over into English, an 'escapade' has become an episode of 'reckless behaviour' (Oxford Compact English Dictionary). Chapter 4 contains many examples of divergence in meaning between signified and signifier; however, Derrida takes this divergence or slippage much further in the concept of polysemia or multiple meanings. Words then take on different meanings as they move through time and cross borders and consequently our word expressions may not carry the same interpretations into the future even for ourselves, since when we reread our own text in the future, we may interpret it differently and want to amend it. This is because our identity has evolved or changed, and we are not exactly the same person with the same interpretation that we had previously held.

Polysemia must be the next step, once it is accepted that there is no necessary internal connection between a word and its meaning given that signification comes about only through association between a phoneme and an object-idea. There is nothing to stop other phonemes becoming associated with an object-idea and when this happens the ones that will prevail will become the main dictionary definition. When one or two meanings prevail then others necessarily become marginalized so that the more dominant meanings can prevail.

Again, this happens through the illusory nature of presence and the presence of sameness in the spoken word, upon which the written word has always historically occurred. Throughout history the power of presence has shaped the meanings of language in the presence of speech, and this has been reinforced through writing to provide permanence and authority. However, this is false and illusory; there is no pure presence because we all live in time which is constantly moving forward, and, as the past folds into the present, the present continuously becomes the past; there is then no time for the present to exist. The present is caught on a knife edge between the past and the future and try as we may, even in moments of triumph we cannot stretch out the present and so all our victories quickly become past successes, subsequently brought to memory in documents or other symbols. However, as already mentioned there is no one single identity existing for all time of people, events, symbols and documents due to this movement through time and the concomitant reinterpretations of words, symbols and events. Derrida names this continued reinterpretation 'deferral' but added to this is 'difference' due to polysemia. Within the apparent sameness of an identity, there is difference and some differences have been suppressed due to a hegemony of identity. However, the suppressed differences remain in the trace which contain the ingredients of deconstruction which as Royle points out, 'makes every identity at once itself and different from itself' (2000; p11).

In the next section, we will focus on how deconstruction brings to the surface-suppressed meanings to present texts with a fuller identity and an ongoing possibility of the 'supplement' containing further developments and reinterpretations in identities going forward into the future.

Power

The exercise of power creates a hegemony in meaning bridging the gap between signifier and signified and this is seen in performative language where power creates an inflated presence and presence of meaning so that when the sergeant-major barks the command 'Stand to Attention' the young private stands to attention. Due to the presence of power, there is not much room for interpretation and the young soldier, even if so inclined, is not likely to reply to the sergeant-major, 'Well that depends on what you mean by "attention"?'. When such performative language is written down for instance in legal text in terms of what will happen if such and such behaviour is not carried out such as not attending school or not meeting bail conditions, then inevitably such written performative text is authoritarian. This is because written text does extend presence giving it a bureaucratic power. However even written text or media images have no absolute presence and in time become historical documents for the archives as time elapses and social context evolves. This can have dangerous implications for humanity as the history of events fades and sometimes it has to be kept alive so that we remember history's tragic events such as the Holocaust and colonial slavery.

For Derrida furthermore, a word has other meanings that have been suppressed in the exercise of power but as already stated, these marginalized meanings leave a trace as one actually privileges a particular meaning over others. It does not mean that these other meanings have ceased to exist but instead they must be revealed in the process of deconstruction. Bush states, 'The trace, for Derrida, is something that is absent but that has left its mark; the trace has effects even when it is no longer present' (2009; p49). Deconstruction is the project to set power aside to uncover marginalized identities and by extension on a larger scale, to uncover marginalized cultural identities which are contained within language use. Where there are traces of other cultures and identities that have been displaced, Derrida asserts that theses traces are the differences that need to be resurrected. Moreover, the ingredients of such deconstruction lie within the provisional and apparent identity of sameness in the text. This again is to reiterate the answer to the question posed earlier on in terms of finding difference within sameness and indeed for Derrida, Sameness and Presence are imposed and, in absolute terms, illusory. They are both subject to unpackaging in order to excavate difference in the process of deconstruction.

Deconstruction

Derrida's project is to expose difference in text using the notion of deferral where meanings can have no finality because of time as ongoing duration. If a written text is sent out into the world, the author's original semantic intention at the moment of writing may well be interpreted differently by the reader in a few months, years or decades into the future. Narrative historical discourses are interpreted and reinterpreted such as for example Wellington's victory at

Waterloo, as a unique British victory. On reinterpretation, it is seen that the national story has marginalized the role of the Prussian army led by General Blucher and in fact the victory was in truth a British-Prussian alliance. Another example is the reinterpretation of the British Colonial Empire in the light of slavery and the Black Lives Matter movement of 2020-1. The reassessment diminishes the glory that this once had enshrined by the erection of statues such as Cecil Rhodes in Oxford. There is now a strong movement to pull these statues down as celebratory monuments and put them in a museum as a reminder of the ignominy of the empire that they represent.

Derrida's project is to deconstruct such hegemonic meanings and part of this is not to allow the signified to retain unquestioned meaning. Indeed, the Derridean idea is that the signified itself becomes a signifier and so meaning or signification always has a forward movement to the future in an endless deferral of meaning. Instead of retaining any meaning the signified has, according to Derrida, the trace of a meaning, of what the meaning once was in the signified. However, this is now absent as the signified no longer holds permanent meaning but becomes a signifier itself. Absence of displaced or suppressed meaning leave a trace to presence because it is an absent presence, an absence with the trace of presence. In everyday life, for example, to vigorously deny something, to deny existence, such as the existence of God reinforces presence, because the assertion of non-existence leaves behind it a trace of the existence one has denied and therefore, by extension, its presence. It can be argued then that God is present through His Absence. Therefore, to state that something is not the case can indeed imply that it is not outside the realms of possibility that it could be the case. Absence being a trace of a presence albeit provisional is not so unusual in daily life since in everyday experience people are often referred to 'as conspicuous by their absence'. So ironically, it is possible at a different level to be present by not being present in that the former presence leaves a gap which is a 'trace' of what once was. ' ... .the deconstructionist demonstrates how the prioritized term requires the excluded term for its intelligibility and operability' (2009; p51).

The principal outcome of this is that there is no such thing as objective and completed absolute meaning. In absolute terms nothing has meaning except by a conventional agreement which of course can always be 'deconstructed'. Spivak (1997) in his preface to Derrida's 'Of Grammatology' highlights the purpose of deconstruction as follows, 'Deconstruction seems to offer a way out of the closure of knowledge' (1997; plxxvii). Further on he asserts, 'No text is even fully deconstructing or deconstructed' (lxxviii). The notion of any transcendental self is questioned, and we are left with what we agree upon intersubjectively as a stable meaning and identity. Yet intersubjectivity is constituted by interpretable words and their temporary meanings. So, in post-structural terms we would refer to identity being a series of unrelated subjectivities as we pass from situation to situation over place and time. The Ricoeur type narrative identity is what we have to piece together ourselves for our own sense of orientation but even this does not possess internal meaning because the ingredients for it are shaped by how the social world has interacted with us and shaped our perceptions, yet again through language. Bush sums up the post-structural situation offered by Derrida as follows, 'So, the meaning of any sign is elusive, constituted by differentiation from other signs, but deferred endlessly, as signs can only be explicated in terms of other signs, and those in turn by other signs' (2009; p50).

This might seem bleak because there is no Godlike magisterium to provide us with a necessary benevolence of meaning and identity in Derrida's world and yet he refers to this deferral of meaning as 'play' in the following statement, 'From the moment that there is meaning, there are nothing but signs. We only think in signs which amounts to ruining the notion of the sign … … … One could call play the absence of the transcendental signified as limitlessness of play, that is to say as the destruction of onto-theology and the metaphysics of presence' (1997; p50). So, there is no metaphysical grounding of meaning in a matrix of signification which says definitively, 'this means this' or 'this means that' and by extension there is no identity, but a series of subjectivities constituted in difference which in turn constitute further differences. Identity then is an interplay between sameness which is always provisional and an intrinsic difference where deconstruction can reveal further difference and so on to the point of singularity and uniqueness.

Further differences going into the future always emerge due to supplementarity because the writer can always add to what has been said or another writer in a different context can add something creating the identity, still provisional, of more difference between the new and the already existing. So, the original has changed, and the new formation will change again. Royle (2003) states that the dynamic of difference and deferral which Derrida names différance (his neologism is spelt with an 'a') is neither a presence nor an absence but a possibility not yet realized. Royle states that 'différance is the splitting, and the deferring of presence and identity' (2003; p76). The corollary for personal identity is that it is always unfinished as we ourselves look to meet ourselves in an unattainable completeness of singularity. This is where we would be our own singular identity, in our unique own difference without comparison with any other sameness. This may seem like the search for individualism in the modern world, yet if this were realized as a presence it would only be provisional, containing within itself the ingredients of its own deconstruction. Royle (2000) states that deconstruction is 'what makes every identity at once itself and different from itself' (2000; p11).

Derrida's solution to the injustice of the power of illusory presence is a new form of writing referred to by him as 'archewriting' which essentially is that life is text and we have Derrida's famous quote that 'there is nothing outside the text' ('il n'y a pas de hors-text'). Presence becomes engulfed in the whole flow of meanings in the totality of the text and eventually disappears. Derrida states as follows, 'And thus to infinity, for we have read in the text that the absolute present, Nature that which words like "real mother" name, have always escaped, have never existed; that which opens meaning and language is writing as the disappearance of the natural presence' (1997; p159). Writing as text, therefore, comes first as does the linguistic system in Saussure, so consequently 'Langue' and not 'Parole'. However, this is a new concept of writing where everything is text and interpretable over time and place and into which presence can merge and vanish. Discourse is, as a result, then forever open-ended and unconstrained since all is open to deconstruction as an ongoing project.

Conclusion – identity or subjectivity

I think we might conclude by saying that a fixed identity such as a narrative identity is not a closed unitary meaning but always open to a search for interpretation in view of potential difference, in terms of other voices which have inserted themselves and also otherness which has been marginalized. We might, on deconstruction, see our seemingly unitary identity as being constituted by different subjectivities which are or have been our lived experiences. From this patchwork we may very well construct a narrative to form a functioning coherent working identity and so, we can have layered personal and social identities. Bush asserts that 'The links between signifiers and signifieds are practically constituted for practical purposes and need only be sufficient for the achievement of the particular aims' (2009; p 56). So, we can use signs in the way we want to use them for our particular practical narratives and then also we can explore them further to expand identities outside these narratives. Consequently, it is not a question of 'either or' but 'both and'. The UK, in its demographic, has multiple identities for belonging if one can see individuals as being for example simultaneously Asian, Scottish and British or Black, Welsh and British. These are then identities which exist at different levels going from more specific to more general and to which one could add European in each case.

At the same time as multiple identities, it is difficult to deny more unitary identities at a more general level since we share a common humanity and internally intelligible forms of language at its core. It does seem that, as Bakhtin argues for both culture as well as for language, that there are centripetal and centrifugal forces where core commonalities exist and yet, layered on top of and around this, are more interwoven levels of identities which are more specific to situations and contexts. There is a specificity and singularity of identity that we recognize in people – for example, I can say that I recognize the identities of my grandson at the general level in that he is a five-month-old baby at the time of writing with all the usual features of being a baby – we can all recognize a baby when we see one due to a common identity and yet within this generality there is a specific identity particular to him in the way he looks at you, his gurgling sound, the features particular to him. I can say the same about my granddaughter who is, at the time of writing, four years of age in that there is specificity in her features, sound and her way of being within the generality of being an infant. If we can acknowledge these features in others of general and singular identity, others can recognize them in us. Royle (2003) writes, 'Everyone has their own way of doing, thinking, feeling or experiencing things: it may be a question of how you choose to pose – or how you find yourself posing – for a photograph; it may be the "singular situation" of having a conversation with someone on a certain fine day, for example, with "the sea on my right"' (2003; p120). Royle refers to Derrida's argument that we are signed by our singular identity within the general and although we are recognized by our uniqueness, it never belongs to us – 'it signs you without belonging to you' (Royle 2003; p120 quoting Derrida). This uniqueness exists in our 'firstness' but escapes us in our 'secondness' in trying to grasp its subjectivity. Again, Royle refers to Derrida saying the desire for the idiomatic (or singularity) 'only appears to the other and it never comes back to you except in flashes of madness … …' (2003; p124). Therefore, our singular identity as a subject cannot be grasped by ourselves as a subject but only as an object of ourselves and so, as we cannot fully master or know ourselves, there is always, as perhaps Bergson would argue, something of the flow of our own being that escapes capture.

Although Derrida does then focus on difference and escaping the gravitational pull of hegemony for reasons of freedom and open-ended interpretations, I think that this book shows so far that identity is about both sameness as well as difference and, moreover, singularity where the person I love is like no other in the world, absolutely unique and yet this is set against the person's generality in terms of a human identity with common human attributes. Such is the nature of identity in its elusiveness, much like the Bergsonian ineffable flow of life and yet recognizable in its object commonality. Identity is then both subject and object, Difference and Sameness.

The next chapter argues for a two-way direction of language and sign as semiotics, both together where meaning is internally as well as externally directed.

9

Signs and Semiotics in Identity

In this chapter, I argue that the identity of signs and their users or interpreters have an externally facing aspect and/or an inward-oriented aspect according to the sign and its interpretation. Here I refer to the sign as having an intrinsic value and or an external exchange value of status or style with the outside world. So, the life of a sign can go inwards to reveal or outwards to transmit or indeed both depending on the position of the 'interpretant', a term coined by the American philosopher C.S. Peirce. I argue in this chapter that sign behaves in the same way as language with an internality revealing knowledge like the properties of geometrical shapes with an a priori intrinsic value and, also external communication. There is a signifier and a signified as in language although as we shall see later in the chapter in the poststructuralist model, a signifier without a signified as one image moves to the next. I focus on Baudrillard in his view of the centrifugal transitoriness of signs which increasingly become a deterministic social environment shaping people's identities. I finish the chapter with an account of critical linguistic analysis to regain a sense of agency in identity in being able to critically analyse the discourses that attempt to shape us.

Peirce used the sign in the same way as Saussure as a signifier pointing to an object as signified; however, he introduced the notion of 'interpretant' as the third element being the person interpreting the sign. For Pierce, the sign is only a sign if there is an interpretant or in other words someone to interpret the sign. Without the interpretant there is no sign. There are then three constituents to a sign: – sign-vehicle, object and interpretant and they are connected as of necessity. As Atkin (2016) points out, 'If we take away any one of the three elements, whatever we are left with is no longer a sign' (2016; p131).

Signs, as communication, are a language and refer to an object outside of themselves – they replace objects in a succinct manner, otherwise explicated in more detail by the symbols of language as words. As already mentioned, in the Saussurean model, there is, in conventional signs, a gap between sign and the object it refers to. So, much like language as words, the language of signs needs to be interpreted by an 'interpretant' and this can have cultural implications; for example, in American, making a circle between the forefinger and thumb means 'great', in French it means 'zero', the opposite of great. In English, showing someone two fingers is an aggressive insult whereas in French, it means nothing beyond denoting a pair. So, confusion can occur because of the separation of signified from signifier in signs.

Types of signs – C.S. Peirce

In Charles Sanders Peirce's classification of signs, they consist of three categories of hierarchically organized signs (Atkin 2016). The most basic and readily accessible type of sign in terms of cognition is the ICON which materially resembles within itself the thing that it represents. A warning road sign showing a deer within a red triangle designates a stretch of road where deer may unexpectedly cross the roadway causing a possible collision. Another warning sign at the roadside shows a cliff face with falling boulders designating a stretch of road where rockfalls may occur. Icons then are simple messages readily understood because of their resemblance to the objects they stand in for. Secondly Peirce defines 'INDEXICAL' signs which point to or index the objects they represent, incorporating something of the iconicity of the icon; however, the most important element is causality where the sign must index the object as its cause. An example of this would be a footprint or a fingerprint. An animal footprint allows the tracker to see iconicity in that it is from an animal being the trace of a hoof or a paw. However, the operational feature is that of causality, in that it has been caused by the object to which it refers. Pierce refers to a 'genuine index' (Rohr 2019) which has both causality and the likeness of the object's trace to which the sign refers. So that in this category the indexical sign incorporates relevant traceable parts of the icon to the object, to which it also points as causality. There is also another subcategory that Peirce designates which is that of the 'degenerate index' which is a general pointing to a close object possible accompanied by saying 'this' or 'that' but with no iconic element.

Finally, we have speech or writing in language which concerns SYMBOLS and bears no resemblance to that which is represented. So, the word 'house' does not look like an object with four walls and a roof, and the word 'car' does not resemble a metal bodywork on four wheels. An exception, in a limited respect to this, is onomatopoeic words which, in some way, resemble sound in their spelling such as 'plop, plop, plop' or dripping water or the 'whoosh' of a blast of wind. However, these are nonetheless developed as words and evolved as vocabulary and may be different in other languages. For example, in English sudden pain prompts onomatopoeic, 'ouch' or 'ow' whereas in French, the onomatopoeic is 'aie' with a trema over the 'i'.

Because Peirce takes the same route as Saussure in separating the signifier from the signified in signs, the meaning gap is bridged by conventional agreement that a certain sign means a certain thing. However, when we come across a rarely used sign, we may ponder as to its meaning and even if some iconicity is present in the sign, the meaning might need some working out. Consequently, we cannot completely rely upon perception but must make inferences by drawing upon previous experiences of signs since the world is full of signs either socially constructed as in road signs or natural. As in sunsets associated with sunny dawns or thunder associated with lightening.

For Pierce as for Bergson, the 'Firstness' of the world escapes us and our understanding cannot fully discern it, so social construction of language and sign is always playing catch-up to gain some cognition of the world and of ourselves. Consequently, the world eludes us in our personal identity, and we have to gain mastery of language and sign as socially agreed in order to encompass who we are. Even so, as we cannot think without signs, we only know ourselves through the way we represent ourselves to ourselves in signs, as word symbols. If this act of representation is undertaken with a lack of accurate vocabulary, perception, knowledge or benevolence in our verbal expression, the risk is of unjustly and unkindly labelling people and also ourselves in a negative way because we will fail to encompass the absolute fullness of their identity. Consequently, the world always exceeds the signs constructed to interpret it. Again, sign includes symbols that constitute words. For Peirce, we are signs to ourselves, we define ourselves through language as 'this' or that' but the social construction of the signs constructed to define ourselves always eludes who we are, and unless there is identity exploration using a specialized language, we, in a casual sense, do not fully know ourselves or others. Popper maintains that 'the self evolves together with the higher functions of language, the descriptive and the argumentative functions' (Popper 1994; p129). By this he means that the more we develop language as word-signs beyond the basic biological behaviourist stimulus–response, the more we develop the linguistic capacity to make ourselves the object of our reflective analysis to explore who we are. This is why Popper refers to higher linguistic functions as argumentative or critical functions. The corollary of this is that those who have a low level of linguistic development are not going to be able to fully explore either their identity or the identity of others. Of course, this makes the case for language-sign education in all sections from nursery and primary school through to secondary school and university.

Nevertheless, Peirce seems to hold to the Kantian view of the world that we do not know the world beyond our own linguistic and perceptive construction of it – we do not have direct knowledge of the world. This lack of directness, of being able to know the object in itself, results in a world of interpretation where the object, being unknowable, is instead interpreted. So, objects are interpretable in a semiotic chain and interpreted by the interpretant who also becomes in him/herself, a sign for interpretation. As mentioned above, this means that language and sign enable us to interpret ourselves as objects of our attention as well as the objects of our regard in the outside world. Atkin (2016) makes two important points as follows: –'… … every interpretant is itself a further sign of the signified object' (2016; p135) and 'interpretants count as additional signs; signs are themselves interpretants of earlier signs' (2016; p136). This semiotic process can go on infinitely into the future where each interpreted sign is a further sign and also stretches back infinitely into the past due to the fact that there is never an original sign input. There can never be a grounded origin for the sign chain because, as for Peirce as well as for Kant, there is no direct objective connection to the world beyond the way in which we see it.

We can never know, for example, an apple in itself but instead the external properties of the apple as signs or, in Peircean terms 'sign-vehicles', which are the salient signs coming to us through perceptive attributes relating to sight, taste, touch, etc. As interpretants are also considered to be signs to others through transmitted 'sign-vehicles' related to qualities of perception, we can never fully know anyone in themselves and therefore identities must remain forever incomplete and transient. So even with a highly developed linguistic ability we can never achieve closure in the knowledge of someone and so completeness in identity of others as well as oneself remains forever elusive. There is a causal connection between the perception and the object, but this is limited to the perception of the interpretant and therefore can never tell us absolutely everything there is to know about someone or something. Our own identities and indeed the identities of others are then signs in terms of the representations we make to ourselves of their sign vehicles or salient operative elements of signs. In practical terms it is often in undertaking something new or something challenging that we learn something of ourselves and of others that we did not previously know – we may discover abilities and attitudes towards aspects of life that were hitherto unknown to us. In this way identities, as well as being never fully known, are also forever unfinished and awaiting some sort of future completion. There is also a downside to this, in that because we do not fully know ourselves, we can be led into a negative view of ourselves through the negative labelling of the powerful and significant other. This has important implications for education in terms of positive developmental explorations of identity and we will discuss this in the final chapter.

Pierce arrives at a more conventional semiotic position in his later philosophy where he does refer to a knowable 'dynamic object' (Atkin 2016; p152) which can be known through conventional agreement through stages of interpretation. However, we can see in his earlier philosophy of infinite semiosis, the beginning of post-structuralism and a Derridean notion of deferral. It seems to me that Pierce's end position is very similar to Saussure in terms of meanings through the majority of people agreeing upon what certain words and signs mean, creating an objectivity of agreement and consensus. Nevertheless, this is not absolute and is based upon an unknowability of the world and a consequent lack of transcendence.

Post-structuralism and structuralism

Post-structuralists do not have a problem with this lack of semiotic transcendence because for them the sign is externally facing, with meaning based on social agreement and generated by power. As Usher and Edwards (1994) point out, to secure meaning even if briefly is to hold power. For post-structuralists, there is no interiority and, in a sense, why should there be because who is to decide what a sign signifies? What authority or final arbiter can one appeal to? Arguments around this can quickly become metaphysical between essentialists who say that, for example, natural signs can reveal a pre-existing knowledge and existentialists-poststructuralists who might claim that even natural signs are constructions made by us into a claim for knowledge because we are limited in the knowledge of the world by our perceptions. Again, we could reply that yes, we perceive rather than know directly but our perceptions surely do relate to something of the world before the perception and therefore with empirical evidence there can be a claim for knowledge, independently of the language used in making the claim. The old adage drawn from a natural sign – 'A red sky at night is shepherds' delight and a red sky in the morning is shepherds' warning' – can be empirically tested with regard to fine weather or rainy weather, respectively. A positive result might indicate that structuralism's essentialist identity tendency – a structure with a centre on the one hand and on the other hand post-structuralism's existential identity without a priori grounding – might both together contribute to identity and knowledge, through perception relating to a real occurrence, then observation of this occurrence and finally empirical testing. Such claims for knowledge based upon empirical evidence however must always remain tentative and provisional, only standing until the data changes or the evidence is falsifiable.

Yet again agreement over empirical data is agreement over our perceptions which does not, in a purist sense, reveal essential substance but rather how the world seems to function at a certain moment in time, according to social perception. Identity is consequently always going to be divided over, on the one hand, substantive essence which, beyond signs, is transcendent and elusive and, on the other, visible signs and behaviours. The notion of sign as far as identity is concerned may well consequently have both something of the 'thing in itself' as well as also its social construction in its extension into the world.

Maritain (1937) pointed out that for mediaeval philosophers, 'A sign manifests or makes known, and it makes known something other than itself, whose place it takes … … ' and further on, 'The ancients drew distinction between the natural sign (signum naturale) and the conventional sign (signum placitum)'.

The idea of making known something other than itself, argues Maritain, is particularly relevant to natural signs because that which is indexed is real and the example, he quotes is smoke which as a natural sign, contains iconicity in that smoke and fire go together as smoke is an integral part of fire, and it points to or indexes fire, as causality, in the same spatial location. So, the signified is real and not an idea due to the internal relation between smoke as a natural sign and fire. The sign here is revelatory, making known and also indexical because of the causal connection between the object and the sign. Because of the index as causality, the smoke sign here is both internal and external – internal because it reveals and external because it communicates.

Maritain, as a Catholic philosopher, argues for a category of sign that contains full presence, without a gap between signifier and signified, in the host in the Catholic sacrament of the Eucharist. For him and for many Catholics who believe in the concept of transubstantiation, the host as bread does not just represent the body and blood of Christ as an external sign, it <u>IS</u> the body and blood of Christ. Catholics believe in a miraculous transformation of the bread or host at the moment of invocation when the priest calls on the Holy Spirit to enter the host, 'like the dewfall'. The host is then transformed and becomes active, prompting the Holy Spirit in the partakers of the Eucharist. This is an exceptional example of how, for Catholics the sign and the object to which it refers, join together in pure being to become one for the faithful, whereas for non-Catholics, the host is a sign indexing Christ where sign and object are materially separate. Because of this theology of miracle, the sign itself is no longer a sign but actively becomes the thing it represents prompting the presence of the Holy Spirit in the faithful. Whether one subscribes to this belief or not, the sign, depending on its nature, can have powerful implications from the moment where it is seen and believed as intrinsically active.

However, even amongst Christians, the Eucharist is a sign that divides opinion and has caused bloody conflict between Catholics and Protestants over history, nonetheless showing that, whatever one's beliefs, signs can carry identities however unstable and also, differences in identity: for the Catholic, an inner identity in the Eucharist, for the non-Catholic Christian an indexical identity pointing to and therefore then in remembrance of a biblical event and finally for the non-Christian an outer sign denoting a categorical social identity. There is then the possibility in the sign for both inner and outer identities.

Maritain also points out a category of 'inverted' sign where a subject who generates a sign reveals him/herself in the sign. An example of this is that someone who uses word-signs to praise or malign someone reveals as much of him/herself in the sign as the person who is referred to by the sign. It would reveal the generous or malicious spirit of the person generating the sign as well as making a statement about the person for whom the sign-word is intended. In all cases so far there is an element of structuralism in terms of the sign having some content because it is associated loosely or closely with an object giving it content even if only socially agreed.

For post-structuralists, however, words and signs can have no essence but rather a continual signification, interpretation and reinterpretation to the point where the sign has its own dynamic life detached from any signified object. For language the proponent of linguistic post-structuralism is Derrida and for signs and images, the main protagonist is Jean Baudrillard.

Post-structural semiotic identity

Jean Baudrillard (2001) demonstrates how signs, in advanced capitalism, have proliferated through advertising, logos, fashion and design, etc. and in doing so have become disconnected from concrete reality in an increasingly stylized world. Given that an object can become a sign, then a designed object becomes a sign of a sign, another step away from the object and then the design brand, such as the three stripes of Adidas becomes a design sign on its own account and therefore a contentless object in its own right. Some time ago it was common to see people wearing logo designed tee shirts which had no meaning other than the logo. In this way Baudrillard sees us living in a world of signs, images and moving images which do not hold any permanent substantive meanings beyond the image itself. The image or the logo eventually becomes its own meaning with its more substantive meaning concealed in the shadows. He views this as a feature of advanced capitalism which has gone beyond technical utility and where more is now required to differentiate between equally performing products in the marketplace. The difference now is the design and the lifestyle this evokes. Sign then has become its own economic currency and can even be divorced from the object itself as a brand name on a tee shirt. In the Coca Cola Christmas adverting, Coca Cola becomes the symbol of Christmas alongside Santa Claus displacing any transcendental event. Indeed, Baudrillard declares that 'Transcendence is at an end' where the sign has replaced the transcendent event of object.

Abbinnette (2008) states, 'For Baudrillard, however, the origin of the simulacrum in the "visible technology of icons" has always threatened to overwhelm the transcendence of the real and to transform the agon of representation into the instrument of limitless performativity' (2008; p78). Abbinnette furthermore quotes Baudrillard as follows: 'in a reference to identity connection to the real world being swamped by virtual reality as … … … an abstract 'subject whose thought, imagination and design are predictable outcomes of the system of simulacra' (2008; p79).

Consequently, in the world of moving images and virtual reality, identities lose the anchorage of stable associations and change from situation to situation. One might say that identities risk becoming different subjectivities in different situations and indeed post-structuralists are more ready to refer to subjectivities rather than identities because they can be viewed as changeable and short-lived. We can see how, in the political situation in the UK in 2020 and 2021, traditional political identities in working class north-east of England in the so-called Labour party 'red wall' have been broken by working people voting Conservative for the first time ever. Traditional industries of shipbuilding and coal mining are no longer holding communities together because these old industries are now defunct and individuals now more isolated and individualistic are more vulnerable to the messaging of political media campaigns. Political media slogans such as 'Get Brexit Done' or in 2020–1 'Build Back Better' are easily understood and readily used to influence people rather than the longer explanations of political science. Consequently, lifestyle and political identities are constructed by media messaging for public consumption against which one can judge one's own current identity for personal improvement and enhancement rather than as part of a community identity.

Baudrillard (2001) laments this state of affairs of identities being unhinged and does not applaud it, saying that it eventually leads to alienation where people no longer have a sense of a grounded and relatively stable identity in community. There is a destruction of the real and a shaky belief in appearance and illusion.

Baudrillard's view of the world is that manufactured identities constructed in images become unfortunately real in a denial of free will as people inhabit online communities. Baudrillard then presents us with a determinism that I believe calls for a critical analysis to gain perspective on an encroaching virtual reality.

A form of critical discourse analysis is a way forward in creating an analytical discourse so that individuals who are living within a virtual world are able to explore this identity through the construction of an analytical identity. Critical discourse analysis as proposed by Fairclough (1989, 1992) and Fairclough and Chouliaraki (1999) is, in terms of its full account, beyond the scope of this book since this is a discipline in its own right asking searching analytical questions such as 'who produces the discourse, why do they produce it and what effect do the producers wish to produce in the consumer?'

However critical analytical language can be referenced in terms of the development of language and sign and how basic level language evolves towards a language of reflection in answer to the questioning of reality as we encounter it daily.

C.S. Peirce (Atkin 2016) helps out in this situation because his view of signs is hierarchical: ICONS, INDEXICAL SIGNS, SYMBOLS. We have already discussed how indexical signs contain at least the relevant part of the icon or the 'sign-vehicle' to the message. However, the highest sign is that which we have spent almost the entire book exploring which is the language of symbols in spoken and written words. The sign may very well communicate directly and succinctly but symbols explicate the sign and as such are in a position to analyse and provide the individual with an analytical identity.

Peircean hierarchy of signs and identity

The most basic sign is the icon, as we have seen, and this is linked with primary perception of the sign corresponding visually with the representation. This is a firstness of perception. Atkin states Firstness is the 'general category of our experience that captures feeling, qualities and potentials' (2016; p297). Secondness is portrayed as 'the general category of experience that captures existence, resistance and reality' (2016; p300). This corresponds to indexical signs that point to causality such as fingerprints at a crime scene. This places the icon into a relational context where one thing causes another. It is a higher form of communication because the icon as indexical is communicating more than itself; it is going beyond itself. Finally, thirdness is portrayed as 'the general category of our experience that captures connection, mediation, synthesis and representation' (2016; p300). 'This is the highest form of communication' because it comments on the causality of interacting elements. It narrates a context of interaction in symbolic form because the constituent elements of thirdness are words, which of course bear no resemblance materially to that which is represented. The word is materially disconnected from its representation as it is not a natural sign like the sunrise announcing the beginning of a new day or the sunset announcing the close of the day. Being disconnected the meanings of the word symbol are no more than associated significations caused through repeated designation by the speaking community. As we have seen word meanings can change laterally but they can also change upwards from material designations to abstract conceptual meanings in line with our conceptual system. We can see this then exactly where the same word can have both a physical meaning and an abstract conceptual meaning as we see in the following examples: issue – either a journal issue number or a problem; jaundiced – either suffering from an ailment yellowing the skin or sceptical/mistrustful; judgement – a judge's or referee's decision or a quality of moral discernment; key – either a shaped metal object used for gaining entry/access or a solution/guide or used as an adjective to denote strategic importance such as 'key workers'; posture – either a physical position that someone holds or a mental attitude towards something. This upward movement from simple sign-identity to more complex symbol-identity is echoed in more recent history by Karl Popper (1994) in his hierarchy of communication and analysis of the relationship between body and mind. Popper is an anti-Cartesian although he uses Descartes mind–body duality in order to argue against this rigid dichotomy. In a similar way to Peirce, he posits a hierarchy of being in the world starting with World One which is physical being such as a table or chair.

Before criticizing Popper by arguing that a table or chair is not purely physical but also a product of mind, we should acknowledge that Popper's Word Two is indeed mind and this interacts with the physical world of World One. The product of this interaction is World Three which is indeed a sociocultural product such as a table, chair or gas cooker and also language in speech, writing, texts and books. So, World Three does contain physical objects but they are the products of an interaction with mind. Therefore, a theatre play or novel is a combination of the physical object of the book and the paper but also the mental world of the plot or narration. Popper presents us with an ongoing dialectic because Word Three acts back on Worlds One and Two in an interaction which then goes forward again to develop the sociocultural product of World Three to make changes and modifications in an evolutionary process. So, we will perhaps end up with a better and more perfectly designed table or chair or a more efficient and ecological cooker no longer powered by fossil fuel, or a new movement in literature. For Popper, World Three is objectivity – it is objective knowledge away and removed from the individual's body and mind and it denies Cartesian duality because it shows how, indeed, body and mind are inseparable since they come together in objectivity as objective products.

Much like Peircean hierarchy of signs, Popper proposes a hierarchy of language to go with this staged dialectical world view. In terms of language, Popper recalls his world view hierarchy as follows with level three at the apex and level one at the base:

3 Products (such as books, stories, myths: language)
2 Dispositions of the organism
1 Physical states

(Popper 1994; p81)

Furthermore, he argues as follows: 'While animal languages do not transcend the regions of dispositions to express dispositional states – the human languages, which are also dispositional, transcend the regions of dispositions and so become the basis for the third world' (Popper 1994; p81).

Language and communication then occupy levels two and three where level two, for Popper, is shared by animals and humans as expressions of dispositions and instinct. These are named the lower linguistic functions, whereas level three is only the preserve of humans and considered as the higher linguistic functions which form the basis for objective knowledge. Within level 3 there is also a two-tier hierarchy which at the lower level Popper names the 'Descriptive or informative function' and the higher level the 'Argumentative or critical function' (1994; p84). Therefore, at the apex of linguistic identity in this model lies critical language leading to objectivity and away from subjective narrative.

We must not forget that Popper is not primarily a linguist but an epistemological philosopher who writes about language as a form of knowledge and so views language as both knowledge and communication. Both he and Peirce argue that language as a symbolic form of communication lies at the top of a hierarchy of communication and for Popper the very summit of this is the language of critical awareness in the construction of objective knowledge.

Consequently, in conclusion, we need to consider identities in this book not just as laterally multiple but also hierarchically or vertically layered where language use is able to encompass analytical discourse to bring within its realm signs and semiotics.

I believe that such models of language bring language back to a more central position of critical analysis, in the development of a language of analysis which poststructuralists may want to see as just another discourse. We have shown however that word meanings do develop the abstract capacity necessary to analyse and it would seem that more research is required into the way in which an analytical identity is shaped. Often school students are for example able to narrate events in chronological order in the history curriculum and may receive good marks for this at a lower level of their education. However, as they move towards 'A' level and a possible university education they need to do more than just narrate. They need to say why such and such happened and what were the outcomes and why this led on to the circumstances which then prevailed. Therefore, they need to develop an analytically discursive language as well as the lower language of narration.

A language of analytical identity

Critical language analysis acknowledges the functions of social power in the attribution of meaning. I have argued that words, not being grounded by anything other than social association, can acquire different meanings including meanings more abstract than their physically material meanings. Exactly how this happens could be a direction for further research into language and conceptualization.

Of course, words combine together to form discourse to produce an overall meaning and, meaning, which is attributed socioculturally, is shaped by the subject positions of those who have the power to be heard within the language they use. All languages, however, seemingly impersonal and official, are after all constructed by someone alone or in a social group. Inevitably language itself is constructed by the subject positions and ideologies of those who use it and when used, this language reinforces the subject positions of the users and, if unquestioned, reinforces the required subject positions of the recipients as listeners or readers, through repetition. However, a language of analysis is able to unpick the layers of meaning to consider the purpose of what is being said, who is saying it and who is the ultimate beneficiary?

Fairclough (1989) argues that critical language analysis is a vital component of literacy and language education, and I will focus more on this as a part of critical pedagogy in the concluding chapter. Fairclough states, 'Children ought to have access to an explicit "model" of language because the development of language capabilities depends on critical language awareness …' (1989; p241). Fairclough argues that education is more than the transmission of knowledge and culture. It is more than the narrative of language, of telling the story of society from one generation to the next, as though it is set in stone, with those at the top always at the top and those at the bottom always at the bottom, thereby transmitting a structural functionalist model of the conservation of social structures.

If those in a collaborative and more critical pedagogy develop language as a critical process of questioning to gain knowledge, then they will develop what Popper (1994) describes as a higher critical and argumentative function of language rather than simply a narrative language. As language shapes the user who uses it, the student using a more critically aware language will construct for him/herself, a more 'critical self-consciousness' (Fairclough 1989; p239).

This then is ultimately a question of identity in a dialectic where, as already argued, the critical language user helps to shape the social situation as well as shaping his/her own identity in the use of the language itself. In the end one need not share the pessimistic nihilist despair of Baudrillard where one is at the mercy of a social world and doomed to live uncritically inside its images. As Foucault states, 'social subjects are shaped by discursive practices, yet (they are) also capable of reshaping and restructuring those practices' (Fairclough 1992; p45).

Conclusion

So, language – identity is not just about multiple identities in a lateral sense but also concerns multilayered identities. Critical discourse analysis takes us outside determinism by deploying an analytical discourse so that we can understand who is producing images and signs and their rationale and motivation for doing so. We can enjoy a film like the Matrix, but with an analytical perspective we can attempt to understand what effect the directors are trying to produce and in doing so we may arrive at a conclusion of perhaps simulation theory. We can then research to find out what this is and debate its validity rather than unquestioningly absorb the film, passively concluding that this must be what life really is. Even if we do not get that far, through questioning and trying to use a questioning language, we are nonetheless attempting to reach an understanding as to what such a film is trying to say. Such an analytical activity is a justification for media studies and philosophy on the school's curriculum and in the final concluding chapter we will discuss the implications of language paradigms and identities for education.

Post-structuralists may well say, in response to critical discourse analysis, that this is simply words analysing words or signs analysing signs or symbols analysing symbols. However, not all words and symbols occupy the same status since some words refer to material objects only, whereas others refer to more complex conceptual items which, as Vygotsky (1986) points out, lead to higher-order thinking. Indeed, the same sign and the same word can have a material meaning and at another level a non-material meaning, as already argued and even a spiritual meaning. However, if we have the linguistic awareness to say that a sign might mean many things and not just the one as a determinant of meaning, we are able, as a consequence, effectively to engage in discursive analytical debate using language as a critical tool. Consequently, the linguistic act of debating the pre-eminence or not of the material sign or the spiritual sign in terms of significance is indeed de facto engaging in an analytical discourse separate from the materiality of the signs themselves. In this way identity is questioned and not locked away inside a particular semiotic.

Questioning that leads to debate is then a vital part of critical identity, eliciting an analytical level of discourse and in the concluding chapter, I argue that it is seen in critical pedagogy as the rationale for education.

The concluding chapter will discuss multicultural and multilingual identities in education as difference and critical pedagogy as a way of achieving this difference within a critical discourse that encompasses both Sameness and Difference.

Conclusion

We have, in the course of the book, explored various paradigms in linguistics, from formal linguistics through to post-structuralism and semiotics. How these paradigms are linked to identity is a fundamental question of the book and can be seen in terms of a dichotomy between the innate on the one hand and the socially learned and constructed on the other. A question that arises therefore is whether or not there are essential characteristics of necessity that are indeed innate that serve as a platform for a subsequent socially acquired or learned language and concomitant identity.

Essentialist core identities are typically Cartesian where Descartes (2008) states that there are structures of the world that are innate to the mind and this explains the constitution of knowledge, of which language is integral as its rational expression. Mind and the external world are, in this way, able to connect so that the mind is necessarily able to make sense of the world. Locke however states in the 'Essay Concerning Human Understanding' (2010–15) that the mind is a 'tabula rasa' or blank slate ready to be filled by our capacity for learning. For Locke therefore we do have an in-built capacity to learn, which one could argue is nonetheless an essentialist structure.

The issue of what we possess as characteristics for language knowledge and use is caught between these two poles of difference between on the one hand an innate language function and on the other an innate ability to learn from a 'blank slate'. The linguistic differences might go forever unresolved save to say that many of these linguistic fundamental positions can be traced back to Cartesian and Lockean philosophies and perhaps this is historically where the innate/socially learned debate needs to start. Descartes proposes a certainty that we only have cognizance of the world because structurally the world is already in our mind, and this is why the mind can read the world. If there were not this connection, the world would be a stranger to us in spite of our attempts to understand it.

Conversely, in terms of mind, Locke presents us with 'tabula rasa' but with an ability to learn. This seems less certain, with regard to language since without a structural antecedent, language acquisition is less of a foregone conclusion; some will learn language, and some will not develop linguistically as well as others, depending on social environment and opportunities where the entire developmental emphasis resides. Locke's position does not contain this mooted innate certainty that all will be well given optimal conditions, whatever these conditions are and however they are defined. There is surely a world of linguistic difference between highly educated young people leaving university having completed higher education and those who have completely missed out on educational opportunity leaving school, as in the past, at fifteen years of age. This uncertainty at the root of identity, which lies at the heart of the 'nature-nurture' debate, is reflected in the ideas of three seminal philosophers who came after Descartes and Locke, and they are Kant, Bergson and Wittgenstein. Uncertainty because they declare that beyond our attempts at intellectualization of the world, what lies beyond is totally outside our control and therefore much of our identity remains unknown.

In the *Critique of Pure Reason*, Kant (1993) speaks of only knowing the world through perception beyond which we can have no access. There are indeed however some 'a priori' exceptions to this in the form of innate items of knowledge not deemed to be humanly constructed such as the properties of geometry and the properties of numbers in maths. Indeed Popper (1994) refers to numbers in terms of 'a priori' knowledge as follows. 'Although numbers are made by us, there are certain things about them which are not made by us, but which can be discovered by us' (1994; p20). Such 'a priori' items within a human constructed numbering system are odd and even numbers and prime numbers divisible only by the number itself and by 1. Humans have then not created or constructed these types of numbers and so they are 'a priori' qualities which are inexplicable within nature and beyond our intellectual explication. This 'a priori' knowledge is something which is a part of the objective world and is beyond our own subjectivity which Kant refers to as the 'Noumenon'. We may guess at it and may say it forms the base of our core reason and subsequent empirical knowledge, but we cannot know it. Centuries later, Wittgenstein said exactly the same thing in the Tractatus when he stated that 'Whereof one cannot speak, thereof one must be silent' and 'The limits of my language mean the limits of my world'.

Both Kant and Wittgenstein hint at an unknown world that we cannot reach and so the noumenon might be a matter for faith as opposed to knowledge.

Consequently, with regard to language and identity, we may well be left in a position where we assume that there must be a necessary essentialist rational platform for language to rest upon, arguing regressively that since we use rationality and rational language it must, of necessity, rest upon a bed of rational innate qualities that are non-linguistic. This seems to be a reasonable 'a priori' reasoning, based on inference, that we possess an innate and inherent structure for the reasoning itself. Chomsky argues that innateness involves a specific 'a priori' language module as an integral part of our innate capacity for learning but this may be impossible to verify empirically, as opposed to being asserted. Most educationalists, in terms of their practice, would regard identity as developmental regardless of innate nature and a current idea is that there are multiple intelligences relating to language, number, artistic ability, physical or kinaesthetic ability, etc. One could argue that there is an ability for each thing we do and the verification of this is existential in terms of the way in which we identify with and then perform the activity. Philosophers such as Kant and Wittgenstein argue that unless we can perceive and then verify in creating in language a true picture of the world, then we do not know. We might assert, we might infer by saying that our rationality in arguments can be extrapolated to a different situation but unless the situation can be verified in perception and in language, we cannot know for sure.

Finally, the third of these philosophers is Bergson who states that we cannot know the world because its flow exceeds our capacity for knowledge. The world exceeds the structures of our intellect. We try to rationalize it but it goes beyond our capacities and our structures. Therefore, the intellectual grasp of language and the world captured by perception and language may well be correct, but this is only playing catch-up and analysing only a fragment of what has already escaped us in its flow.

However, we should not ignore rational identity and the internal intelligibility of language that we apprehend just because we cannot grasp the vastness of life and communication outside our intellectual grasp.

Identity within mind

We have seen in Chapter 1 that Chomsky argues for the internal rationality of language in terms of grammar. For Chomsky grammar is not communication but knowledge. Unlike systemic functional linguistics, the formal linguistics of Chomsky does not address social communication and in this sense Chomskyan

Universal Grammar is a grammar of the mind and linguistics is a branch of psychology. Chomsky does not engage in empirical proofs of his grammatical thesis and does not look across a range of unrelated languages to ascertain the basic commonalities of all grammars. Indeed, criticism is directed against him for his lack of empiricism although I think it should be accepted that he is not a linguist since he does not comment on the application of languages in general nor on the semantics of language but is instead a philosopher of language. Chomsky simply asserts that we have a basic rationality and shows, through the medium of English, how this has to make sense internally so that we can read each other. Chomsky in this sense is a linguistic exponent of Descartes in terms of language as knowledge. The assertion is that sentences have to hold together in being intelligible and these verbal expressions are integral to a rational mind. Therefore, the grammar is in the mind and comes to the surface in the words and sentences we utter. Because of this, we are able to translate in and out of different languages due to rational commonalities, although it does need to be acknowledged that much can be lost in translation due to linguistic cultural differences embedded in word meanings.

We see in the book that word order is a basic linear grammar. However, this develops into more complicated structures when phrases and sentences join together through grammatical mechanisms such as relative adjectives and pronouns, so that in a sentence such as 'The car that I bought was expensive', the object of the sentence 'the car' comes before the subject 'I'. Word order can then change but, because of the rationality of grammar the sentence can still be rational as long as grammatical mechanisms allow for this. In Chapter 1 for instance, we see that word order in Basque is very different from English or French but the strategic position of each word, as opposed to the physical position, is flagged up in the case ending of the word to make for rational intelligible utterances.

In Chapter 2 on cognitive linguistics, we see how semantic possibilities are developed within conceptual structures in the mind in a different location to language and these two areas join together to produce meaning. Vygotsky (1986), within a socio-linguistic and cultural paradigm of language, supports this view of conceptual structure as initially separate from language, coming together with language to form a dialectical relationship for the development of higher-order thinking. In this way conceptual resources in the form of images, metaphors and spatial relationships join with words to form word-images. The close association due to frequency of use between phonemes or word-sounds joining together with word-images means that the utterance of the word can instantly reproduce the image-meaning and, words, as a consequence, are used to produce meaning and construe the world. Performative linguistics, through the use of power, can command social aspects of the world into existence. An act of parliament in its verbal construction contributes powerfully through the law to required behaviour and a judge, in his/her verbal pronouncement, enacts the law in pronouncing a sentence which is fairly immediately enacted physically. From this we can see that identity is also constituted intersubjectively in sociocultural interaction and can be shaped by power behind and within language. Cognitive linguistics takes into account the sociocultural as well as the rational aspects of identity since images and metaphors are culturally constructed in the inter-subjective mind.

Intersubjectivity

We can see the different aspects of identity as we change our emphasis on language, from language and grammar of the mind towards sociocultural language and identity. For example, metaphors and images are cultural and we can see that there are linguistic metaphors in English that do not exist in another language such as French. In an informal online linguistics discussion I was engaged in, I researched a French translation of the English metaphor 'To soldier on'. This is a frequent everyday metaphor signalling an uphill struggle perhaps against prevailing adverse conditions with the image of a soldier pushing on in the face of adversity. A French translation is 'persévérer' and this is intelligible within the word meaning but it does not contain the above image or picture. Someone who learns English will take on this image and this might enhance an intersubjective cultural understanding which is a benefit of foreign language learning. The cultural dynamics of the social and cultural world therefore enter into language through the conceptual system making language and identity more than just mental characteristics but also sociocultural features. This interplay between the personal and the social, between the internal of language and its externally facing social nature means that we can use language to explore our own identities in making ourselves the object of our own analysis based on the social world as we have experienced it. The consequence of this is that we can explore our own identities and develop them further through our own exploration of different sociocultural environments and educational experiences.

The 'Other' in terms of the social world we encounter beyond ourselves is necessarily integrated to our identity through heteroglossia as proposed by Bakhtin (1981) where the language and discourse of others including interlocutors come to be interwoven in our own utterances. This could include something as simple as identification with a television media advert by singing the 'jingle' which is something advertisers would wish us to do in repeating their adverts through identification with the product.

Bakhtin (1981) then argues that our language exists in a thread arising from what others have said in interaction with us and this includes education, media and interlocutors. We process this raw material and pass our version of it onto others and if our voices are powerful ones there is a chance our interlocutors or readers will repeat much of what we have said, perhaps incorporating our verbal material into their developing identities.

Identities are then intersubjective and often shot through with the voices of powerful others. For instance, long before s/he is in a position to verify statements a young child will repeat items of knowledge imparted by the teacher such as 'Canberra is the capital of Australia'. Less authoritative voices might say otherwise such as Sidney or Melbourne, but the child is taught respect for the voice of the teacher and so the authority of her/his voice is likely to prevail, and this authoritative voice carries with it knowledge power. Alternative voices may challenge official knowledge-power and, as a result, challenge expert voices with an alternative reality which does not have epistemological grounding. An example of this is that at the time of writing, September 2021, there is controversy in some areas concerning vaccinations and mask-wearing during the Covid-19 pandemic. Some voices which tend to be largely on the margins of society, although also present to a lesser degree in the mainstream, argue against masks and against vaccines in the name of liberty and vaccine safety. More recently there have been demonstrations every Saturday in Paris and other French cities against the 'Covid Pass' proving that one has been vaccinated so that one can gain entry into certain public places and to retain certain jobs. Much of this rebellion against mainstream scientific views has been fostered on the internet and social media platforms which mainstream science has criticized as 'fake news' or disinformation. These controversies raise issues of knowledge and power in terms of who has the voice powerful enough to be heard and believed. The mainstream media carries the government's message supported by the scientific and medical community that mask-wearing and vaccinations are extremely important to preserve life and prevent serious illness, yet in spite of this people who are 'anti-vaxx' and 'anti-mask' believe that they are being lied to and that there is a conspiracy to deny freedom; even that the disease does not exist or is not dangerous. They believe they have the true knowledge in saying that Covid is about as dangerous as influenza and so there is a conflict as to where knowledge lies. So, Foucault's claim then that power carries knowledge has merit, but of course the problem occurs where knowledge identity is based on hearsay or popular voices holding sway which are epistemologically unfounded so that for example in this Covid pandemic in 2021 people might believe that life-saving vaccinations are harmful in some way and restrictive of freedom due to Covid passport checks. Therefore, there is a power battle for knowledge and even though knowledge claims are epistemologically supported by science they are not believed in some quarters. I think that this does support the Foucauldian claim that power and knowledge are closely interrelated.

Our identities are then interwoven with others for good or ill and, as we will argue, later in this chapter, that this has important implications for education insofar as cultivating a philosophy of critical pedagogy and critical awareness of what others tell us.

The notion of power is extremely important in our construction of belief systems, in terms of what we take for knowledge and concomitant identity, especially where there is negative labelling in institutions such as family, church, education, care settings which could lead to abuse.

Bakhtin argues that language and consequently identity exist and come into play in the interface between oneself and the Other. So, the 'Other' is an alterity, an identity that we do not fully know.

Identities and subjectivities

Post-structuralists tend to refer to subjectivities since individuals experience many different social settings including online social media platforms and so they argue that there is not one hegemonic single unitary grounded identity but lots of changing subjectivities as individuals move from situation to situation. People construct themselves from all the different discourses they traverse and are able to form different opinions of themselves. A critical observation might be that people suffer from fractured identity in a decentred world although a post-structuralist may well contend that such a variety of available discourses make for individual agency with people picking and choosing which identities to adopt. Consequently, an individual need not be trapped by a negative identity if s/he can explore other subjectivities in different contexts. Again, this has strong implications for education and pedagogy in terms of a curriculum that can support identity exploration such as modern foreign language (henceforth MFL) learning and other humanities and arts subjects, which one can argue are liberating areas of the curriculum.

I believe there is a case for interaction and negotiation between subjective experience in its 'firstness' and a more continuing notion of identity serving as a modifiable platform on which subjectivities are based. This recalls Ricoeur's notion of an ongoing stable identity of 'idem' modifiable by the future becoming version of identity as 'ipse', therefore identity as product and identity as process; Sameness in identity and the encounter with Difference and also the Future as two alterities. A perspective is needed across linguistic paradigms to reconcile these versions of identity from the rational mind-based centralizing identity to the wider more exploratory and creative aspects of identity. Here we are beginning to see emerging the two alterities of identity – firstly the 'Other' beyond ourselves and secondly, within the course of book, the future in terms of our becoming, which also lies beyond ourselves.

Chapter 7 on Ricoeur shows how an ongoing narrative identity can be constructed to integrate disparate subjective experiences into a coherent framework which in contemporary life is the core function of CV's or to a much wider extent biographies, autobiographies and autobiographical novels such as the classic French opus by Marcel Proust over seven volumes titled 'A la Recherche du Temps Perdus' – 'In Search of Lost Time'. An example of a more rational language overseeing the 'firstness' of an emotional subjective experience can be seen in the following text by Jane Austen in her novel 'Persuasion', where after eight years the main protagonist Anne Elliot experiences an emotional reacquaintance with Captain Wentworth with whom she had had a romantic attachment. Austen writes,

> She had seen him. They had met. They had been once more in the same room! Soon, however, she began to reason with herself, and try to be feeling less. Eight years, almost eight years had passed, since all had been given up. How absurd to be resuming the agitation which such an interval had been banished into distance and indistinctness
>
> (J. Austen p56 Persuasion. Penguin Classics 1998)

We see in this passage an attempt to reconcile and rationalize her 'idem' identity with an emotional subjective experience, suggesting that there is an ongoing language of stable continuous identity into which the subjective experience of becoming can be integrated. A language of critical analysis would need to make the distinction between the language of narrative first-hand experience in terms of a happening or occurrence and a second analytical language of reflection on the event.

Therefore, we refer here to a layered language where occurrence occurs first in our encounter with alterity or otherness, followed by a language of 'secondness' taking in context and 'thirdness' which takes a higher perspective of overview or an encompassing analysis constructing a reflective identity. The reflective identity develops a language of critique – looking at an event's purpose, wider justification, its moral outcome and future consequences. We saw in Chapter 7 that a more intellectually constructed narrative identity has to encompass the first-hand experience of alterity or otherness. There are events in life that are unexpected which come along to disrupt whom we think we are. When we open ourselves up to a new day or new people, we encounter alterity and new possibilities for identity, which need to be reconciled with continuing identity using a more reflective discourse.

Voices and identities

If we take Bakhtin's perspective that both language and culture have a centrifugal movement as well as a centralizing one, we need to combine language and identity as rational and analytical together with language and identity as expansive and exploratory in terms of different cultures and future possibilities. The latter is a case to be argued for in favour of differences in voices and identities and the notion of alterity. A case therefore in education for multiculturalism and multilingualism. There is evidence that people in multilingual settings draw upon language as a resource to cater for their cultural needs. The practice of drawing upon different language at their disposal to say different things in different languages within the same conversation is known as 'translanguaging' (Garcia 2009) and shows a flexibility and openness in cultural identity.

These two apparently opposed notions of language as centrally rational and at the same time as culturally expansive are perhaps two sides of the same coin of Sameness and Difference and not mutually exclusive within the subject area of linguistics. They both have implications for education and development for individuals as we see, as follows, in Dewey's and Schon's differing notions of reflection.

Education, pedagogy and curriculum

Hébert (2015) refers to John Dewey's concept of reflective thinking as a mode of rational analysis of practical situations. This is further developed by Schon who proposes 'knowledge in action' (2015; p364) which arises from reflection in action, which is 'thinking about doing something while doing it' (Hébert 2015; p365). The perspective of these reflective models is Cartesian in terms of the mind–body dualism. Schon, it is argued by Hébert, is less Cartesian than Dewey because his version of reflective thinking is 'in situ' in the event whereas Dewey's is outside the event itself. Nevertheless, both models of analytical reflection are mind-based identities reflecting on subjective experience. In Dewey's case the perspective is reflective after the situation as opposed to within it, using technical-rational language.

This calls for an analytical language to examine ideas either contemporary or historical and I would argue here that this has implications for the secondary school curriculum with regard to study in the social sciences such as sociology, philosophy, critical thinking and in the humanities in history and media studies in particular. Such reflective analytical discourse would in effect reflect upon the moral implications and consequences of events and the motivational forces behind events, calling upon a more questioning critical pedagogy. Guilherme (2015) refers to Paolo Freire's notion of dialogical education which is the 'continuous, critical and dialogical insertion of individuals into their historical context while truly believing in the transformative powers of human agency ...' (2015; p134). This has implications for language and identity in that it is through the critical language of debate and dialogue that a questioning and analytical identity is constructed as opposed to the alternative 'banking' of knowledge. As Evans (2016) points out, Freire advocates a problem-posing model of education where social reality is problematized so that hidden agendas can be made visible and subject to critical analysis.

Therefore, knowledge does not come packaged but instead can be constructed by students and teachers to see how factual knowledge has come to be the way it is. Assumptions can be questioned and the packaging of items of knowledge into conventionally accepted facts through notions of power can be exposed. Alternative considerations for knowledge claims can be explored to attempt to grasp different views of reality such as for example accepted historical facts which have been conventionally constructed through the eyes of the colonizers in colonial history.

Such an approach has developmental consequences for individuals in shaping a questioning identity and is promoted by a critical analytical language from the area of Critical Discourse Analysis and also post-structural deconstruction.

There are subjects that offer a more expansive and creative view of education as opposed to an analytical one and these also have implications for the development of identity. Such subjects that can be included in a literary and creative curriculum that explores identity are Modern Foreign Language (MFL), English and the creative performing arts of dance and drama.

Evans (2015) argues for a concept of otherness or alterity as a rationale for MFL (Modern Foreign Language) education where identities of alterity are explored. Philosophically Derrida (1967) and Levinas (1989) provide the foundational grasp of the 'Other'. Derrida states, 'Face à face avec l'autre dans un regard et une parole qui maintiennent la distance, cet être-ensemble comme séparation précède ou déborde la société, la collectivité. Levinas l'appelle religion. Elle ouvre l'éthique. La relation éthique est une relation religieuse' (Derrida 1967; p142).

'Faced with the other in regard and in speech which maintain distance, this being-together as a separation precedes or transcends society, collectivity. Levinas calls it religion. It opens up ethics. The ethical relationship is a religious relationship' (author's translation).

As Bakhtin argues, language, meaning and culture reside in the border between oneself and the 'Other' and so when one learns a foreign language one necessarily explores the identity of the 'Other' or alterity. One learns identities other than one's own, whose distance to which Derrida refers is always maintained and respected. Both the 'rapprochement' and the maintenance of distance are essential in the valorization of alterity, otherwise there is a danger of colonization, where one sees the other only through one's own eyes and does not attempt to see alterity, and subsequently oneself, through the eyes of the 'Other'. Learning the language of another culture is important to view the 'Other' on his/her own terms because culture resides in the language one speaks/learns in order to access more fully the culture around the language. Traditional tourism through travel companies misses out this language-culture connection and so the alterity one could have found is objectified, since it is assimilated into one's own language-culture. It then becomes a form of colonization where even the foreign words and name places are mispronounced as an English name-word in the case of British commercial tourism.

Consequently, faced with alterity there is, in terms of identity exploration, a continual interplay between the sameness of identity and difference. Alterity is then elusive and needs to be explored through language if it is to remain the 'Other'. We are then able to recognize the sameness with ourselves in terms of common humanity and perhaps also common cultural areas of sameness such as technology and even the sociopolitical environment and then this backdrop of sameness provides a framework for focusing on difference. Language-culture, and that includes the culture that resides within the language in its grammar and lexis, holds the nature of alterity which the learner explores, thereby expanding the borders of his/her own identity without encroaching upon the identities of the 'Other'. Within the relationship between Sameness and Difference, there is a paradox in that one cannot have difference without a framework of sameness, because difference needs to be difference from something and in the same way one cannot have the 'other' without 'oneself' or in terms of Ricoeur, no ipse without idem. Grammatically the identity of 'you' is such because it is differentiated from the identity of 'I', so there is no 'you' without 'I'.

At a deep level, this acknowledgement and valorization of alterity expresses a spirituality in education and development because of this interconnectedness between self and other based on the grammatical relationship between the identities of you and I. Following from this, both linguistic diversity and unity join together where, in bilingual and multilingual situations, language is used as a resource such as in the concept and practice of 'translanguaging' (Garcia 2009). We have the ability in translanguaging to alternate at will between languages which may be both one's own language and the language of the other.

The next section explores how this works within a framework of an underlying universal grammar. Paradoxically I argue that the journey of language and identity from being a rational mind-based centre towards a culturally dispersed dynamic at surface level comes full circle in the concept and practice of translanguaging and multilingual universal grammar. These two concepts allow the structures of grammatical sameness and difference in the diversity of language to join together.

Multilingual universal grammar as difference and sameness in language

Cook (2009) argues that the mind is hard-wired for language in general and that children, as they acquire language, will acquire all the different languages to which they are exposed. Consequently, Cook interprets Chomsky's process of language acquisition for many in multilingual settings rather than just for one language. She quotes examples of people growing up using two or more languages simultaneously instead of the notion of acquiring a native tongue and then consecutive additional languages. In interviews she quotes multilingual language users who did not regard any one of their languages as the native one but acquired all of them simultaneously. She claims that language acquisition is about language irrespective of what language is involved, and it could be any number of languages. Monolinguals are the way they are because they have never had another language available to them, and so they are language deprived.

The mechanisms of acquisition, however, are such that, although children are acquiring language rather than languages, they do manage to keep them apart, assigning different grammatical features to the correct language. Cook maintains that this is due to the Chomskyan grammatical principle of parameters. According to Chomsky, as we have seen in Chapter 1, parameters are grammatical settings that provide for a limited variation in surface grammar. The parameters are a Universal Grammar principle guiding the grammar into usage. They provide for variation and, at the same time, restriction so that there are word formations that are grammatically acceptable and those which are not acceptable. For example, there are parameters which allow for variation in whether or not subject pronouns are used as they are in French and English but not used in Spanish or Italian or whether the adjective comes after the noun as in French, Spanish, Italian or before as in English and German. Therefore, word orders have some freedom of movement so long as they express an underlying grammatical rationale. Consequently, the grammars of bilinguals and multilinguals are acquired simultaneously and continuously across languages within the parameters provided by UG.

Due to conceptual unity beneath the surface differences, multilinguals and bilinguals are able to codeswitch with ease or, to be more exact, translanguage. Codeswitch implies that the two languages are self-contained and so the user goes between two different languages whereas translanguaging (Garcia 2009) denotes a continuation of language with different varieties which users can draw upon as required according to their needs. In translanguaging one could mix languages within utterances because of an underlying conceptual coherence, even though there is surface grammatical variation between languages. Translanguaging, rather than codeswitching, acknowledges linguistic continuity across languages. So, in multilingual universal grammar we see both sameness and difference operating at the same time. Sameness is found in underlying structural coherence and yet, at the same time, difference is found in how this coherence diversifies at surface level into different operational grammars through the principle of parameters.

Sameness and difference have then been the underlying and surface themes running throughout this book both in the identity of language and the identities of language users and in both cases, we find sameness at the centre and differentiation in the external facing cultural contexts.

We have also seen the development of a linguistic metaidentity which serves as an analytical tool to make a coherent sense of difference in language and identity. This analytical identity is actively philosophical in asking questions and especially as critical pedagogy where knowledge is constructed in the process of questioning. The classroom teacher asks questions, not because s/he does not know the answers and needs to find out from the students but in order for the students to 'scaffold' their own knowledge and take ownership of it.

As we saw in Chapter 1, the linguistic metaidentity was also formulated in translating between languages to resolve meanings in encountering different word orders. In this case one has to call upon conceptual structures in an identity overarching the languages themselves in order to analyse meaning, especially when knowledge of one of the languages is limited.

Therefore, the paradigms of language within linguistics are at the root of all levels of identity as this book has attempted to demonstrate and if we did not have language and moreover in its different models, we would have only a vague sense of ourselves founded upon basic instincts and without self-awareness of differentiated identities. We would not have the language either to gain understanding of others, nor the conceptual development through language to develop our own higher-order more abstract thinking.

The different linguistic paradigms are then important for differentiated identities, and I hope this book has demonstrated that they indeed complement each other in gaining an understanding of these different aspects of identity. However, they do need to be able to read each other as aspects of the same subject of linguistics rather than as their own separate linguistic subjects. As Hahn et al. (2020) point out, 'Understanding what is universal and what varies across human languages is a central goal of linguistics' (Hahn et al. 2020, vol. 117 no. 5, PNAS, Stanford University). Seen in this way linguistics can become joined up in its diversity across its different branches. Identity can then be seen in the round as holistic in its many constituent aspects both at the same time as Sameness and Difference, the latter interspersed with both the alterity of the 'Other' and with that of the future in its unfinished identities of becoming.

References

Abbinnette, R. (2008) The Spectre and the Simulacrum. In History after Baudrillard. Theory, Culture & Society Vol 25 no 6 pps 69–87.
Ahmed, A. (2011a) Ludwig Wittgenstein. Philosophical Investigations in Barry Lee (ed) Philosophy of Language. Bloomsbury Publishing.
Ahmed, A. (2011b) Ludwig Wittgenstein. Tractatus Logico-Philosophicus in Philosophy of Language; Barry Lee (ed). Bloomsbury Publishing.
Akamajian, A. (1995) Linguistics: An Introduction to Language and Communication. Cambridge, MA: MIT Press.
Almon, R.L. (2017) The Postmodern Self in Theological Perspective: A Communal, Narrative, and Ecclesial Approach. In Ecclesiology Vol 13 no 2 pps 179–96.
Ansell-Pearson (2018) Bergson Thinking beyond the Human Condition. London: Bloomsbury Publishing.
Atkin, A. (2016) Peirce. London: Routledge.
Austen, J. (1818) Persuasion. London: Penguin Classics.
Austin, J.L. (2011) Philosophy of Language. G.Longworth. (B.Lee. ed). London: Continuum.
Bache, C. (2010) Hjelmslev's Glossematics: A Source of Inspiration to Systemic Functional Linguistics? In Journal of Pragmatics Vol 42 no 9 pps 2562–78.
Bakhtin, M (1981) The Dialogic Imagination: Four Essays. M. Holquist (ed). Austin: University of Texas.
Baudrillard, J. (2001) Impossible Exchange. London and New York: Verso.
Bavali and Sidighi (2008) Chomsky's Universal Grammar and Halliday's Systemic Functional Linguistics: An Appraisal and Compromise. In Journal of Pan-Pacific Association of Applied Linguistics Vol 12 no 1 pps 11–28.
Bergson, H. (1998) Creative Evolution. New York: Dover Publications Inc.
Bhabba, H. (1994) The Location of Culture. London: Routledge.
Bosman, N. (2019) The Cup as Metaphor and Symbol: A Cognitive Linguistic Perspective. In Theological Studies Vol 75 no 3. a5338 https://doi-org/10.4102/hts.v75i3.5338
Bourdieu, P. (1991) Language and Symbolic Power. Cambridge, MA: Harvard University Press.
Bush, S. (2009) Nothing Outside the Text: Derrida and Brandom. In Contemporary Pragmatism Vol 6 no 2 pps 45–69.
Charlton, W. (2014) Metaphysics and Grammar. London: Bloomsbury Publishing.

Charmé, S. (1977) The Two I-Thou Relations in Martin Buber's Philosophy. In The Harvard Theological Review Vol 70 nos 1–2 pps 161–73.

Chevalier and Planté (2016) What Gender Owes to Grammar; Linguistic Analysis and the Study of Language Use Is Thus a Necessary Step in Understanding How the Social Organization of Sex Relations Is Perpetuated. in CCCB LAB, Centro de Cultura Contemporanea de Barcelona. lab@cccb.org.

Chomsky, N. (1968) Languages and Mind. New York, NY: Harcourt Brace Jovanovich.

Chomsky, N. (1975) Reflections on Languages. New York, NY: Random House.

Chomsky, N. (1976) On the Nature of Language. In Annals of the New York Academy of Sciences Vol 280 no 1 pps 46–57.

Chomsky, N. (1980) Rules and Representations. New York, NY: Columbia University Press.

Chomsky, N. (1995) The Minimalist Program. Cambridge, MA: MIT Press.

Chomsky, N. (2009) Cartesian Linguistics: A Chapter in the History of Rationalist Thought. Cambridge: Cambridge University Press.

Chomsky, N. (2011) Language and Other Cognitive Systems. What Is Special about Language? In Language Learning and Development Vol 7 No 4 pps 263–78. Massachusetts Institute of Technology, USA.

Chouliaraki, L. and Fairclough, N. (1999) Discourse in Late Modernity: Rethinking Critical Discourse Analysis. Edinburgh: Edinburgh University Press.

Cook, V. (2009) 'Chapter 3. Multilingual Universal Grammar as the Norm' in Yan-kit Ingrid Leung (ed) Third Language Acquisition and Universal Grammar. Bristol, Blue Ridge Summit: Multilingual Matters pps 55–70.

Cook, V. and Newson, M. (2007) Chomsky's Universal Grammar; an Introduction. Oxford: Wiley-Blackwell.

Crowley, P. (2003) Paul Ricoeur: The Concept of Narrative Identity, the Trace of Autobiography. Edinburgh: Edinburgh University Press.

Derrida, J. (1967) Of Grammatology. Baltimore: Johns Hopkins University Press.

Derrida, J. (1967) L'ecriture et la différence. Paris: Éditions du Seuil.

Derrida, J. (1978) Writing and Difference, trans. A. Bass. London: Routledge.

Descartes, R. (2008) Meditations on First Philosophy, trans. M. Moriarty. Oxford: Oxford University Press.

Dornyei, Z. and Ushioda, E. (2009) Motivation, Language Identity and the L2 Self. Clevedon: Multilingual Matters.

Echeruo, M.J.C. (1995) Derrida, Language Games, and Theory. In Theoria Vol 86 October pps 99–116.

Edwards, R. (1998) Mapping, Locating and Translating: A Discursive Approach to Professional Development in Studies in Continuing Education. Vol 20. London: Publisher Taylor and Francis pps 23–38.

Edwards, R. and Usher, R. (1994) Post-modernism and Education. London: Routledge.

Evans, D. (2015) Language and Identity; Discourse in the World. London: Bloomsbury.
Evans, D. (2018) Language, Identity and Symbolic Culture. D. Evans (ed). London: Bloomsbury Publishers.
Fairclough, N. (1989) Language and Power. London and New York: Longman.
Fairclough, N. (1992) Discourse and Social Change. Cambridge: Polity Press.
Foucault, M. (1972) The Archaeology of Knowledge. London: Routledge.
Foucault, M. (2002) The Order of Things. Abingdon: Routledge.
Garcia, O. (2009) Bilingual Education in the 21st Century: A Global Perspective. Oxford: Wiley-Blackwell.
Giardiello, P. (2018) Youth Identities: Media Discourse in the Formation of Youth Identity in D. Evans (ed) Language, Identity and Symbolic Culture. London: Bloomsbury Publishing pps 85–101.
Guilherme, A. (2015) Indigenous Languages, Cultures and Communities in the Amazon: Strengthening Identities in D. Evans (ed) Language and Identity; Discourse in the World. London: Bloomsbury Publishing pps 123–42.
Gumperz, J. (1999) On Interactional Sociolinguistic Method in S. Sarangi and C. Roberts (eds) Talk, Work and Institutional Order. Discourse in Medical, Mediation and Management Settings. Berlin and New York: Mouton de Gruyter pps 453–72.
Hahn, M., Jurafsky, D. and Futrell, R. (2020) PNAS, Vol 117 no 5 California: Stanford University.
Halliday, M.A.K. (1985) An Introduction to Functional Grammar (1st ed.). London: Edward Arnold.
Halliday, M.L.K. (2002) On Grammar. London: Continuum.
Halliday, M.L.K. (2003) On Language and Linguistics. London: Continuum.
Hart, C. (2014) Discourse, Grammar and Ideology; Functional and Cognitive Perspectives. London: Bloomsbury Publishing.
Heidegger, M. (1993) Basic Writings. New York: Routledge.
Hébert, C. (2015) Knowing and/or Experiencing: A Critical Examination of the Reflective Models of John Dewey and Donald Schön. In Reflective Practice Vol 16 no 3 pps 361–71.
Holvoet, A. (2020) Sources and Pathways for Non-directive Imperatives. In Linguistics Vol 58 no 2 pps 333–62.
Hussein, B.A. (2012) The Sapir-Whorf Hypothesis Today in Theory and Practice. In Language Studies Vol 2 no 3 pps 642–6.
Jackendoff, R. (2007) Language, Consciousness, Culture. Cambridge, MA: MIT Press.
Jackson, H. and Amvela, E.Z. (2007) Words, Meaning and Vocabulary: An Introduction to Modern English Lexicology. London: Continuum.
Jansen, H. (2015) Time, Narrative and Fiction: The Uneasy Relationship between Ricoeur and a Heterogenous Temporality. In History and Theory: Studies in the Philosophy of History Vol 54 no 1 pps 1–24.

Kant, E. (1993) The Critique of Pure Reason. Vasilis Politis (ed). London: Everyman.
Kemmener, D. (2015) Cognitive Neuroscience of Language. New York and London: Psychology Press.
Kramsch, C. (1998) Language and Culture. Oxford: Oxford University Press.
Kumar, R. and Yunus, R. (2014) Linguistics in Language Education. In Contemporary Education Dialogue Vol 11 no 2 pps 197–220.
Lakoff, G. (1987) Women, Fire and Dangerous Things: What Categories Reveal about the Mind. Chicago: The University of Chicago Press.
Lakoff, G. (2012) Explaining Embodied Cognition Results. In Topics in Cognitive Science Vol 4 pps 773–85.
Langacker, R.W. (1987) Foundations of Cognitive Grammar. Volume 1 Theoretical Perspectives. Stanford, CA: Stanford University Press.
Langacker, R.W. (1999) Grammar and Conceptualization. New York: Mouton de Gruyter.
Lee, B. (2011) Philosophy of Language. London: Bloomsbury Publishing.
Lenneberg, E. (1967) Biological Foundations of Language. New York: Wiley.
Levinas, E. (1989) The Levinas Reader. Oxford: Blackwell.
Locke, J. (2010–2015) An Essay Concerning Human Understanding: Book 2- Ideas. Jonathan Bennett. www.earlymoderntexts
Longworth, G. (2011) Philosophy of Language. Barry Lee (ed.). London: Continuum.
Macha, J. (2015) Wittgenstein on Internal and External Relations: Tracing All the Connections. London: Bloomsbury Publishing.
MacSwann, J. (2017) A Multilingual Perspective on Translanguaging. In American Educational Research Journal Vol 54 pps 167–201.
Maritain, J. and Morris, M. (1937) Sign and Symbol. In Journal of the Warburg Institute Vol 1 no 1 pps 1–11.
Marshall, J.D. (1999) Performativity: Lyotard and Foucault through Searle and Austin. In Studies in Philosophy and Education Vol 18 pps 309–17.
Mills, S. (2003) Michel Foucault. London: Routledge.
Moriarty, M. (2008) Meditations on First Philosophy; with Selections from the Objections and Replies. Rene Descartes. Oxford: Oxford University Press.
Ochs, E. (2012) Experiencing Language. In Anthropological Theory Vol 12 no 2 pps 142–60.
Oyhamburu, P. (2011) L'Euskara, la langue basque. Clermont Ferrand: Centre France Livres SAS.
Perlina, N. (1984) Bakhtin and Buber: Problems of Dialogic Imagination. In Studies in Twentieth and Twenty-First Century Literature Vol 9 no 1 pps 13–28.
Popper, K.R (1994) Knowledge and the Body-Mind Problem; In defence of interaction. M.A Notturno (ed). London and New York. Routledge.
Proust, M. (1981) Remembrance of Things Past; Guermantes Way, trans C.K. Scott Moncrieff and Terence Kilmartin. London: Chatto & Windus and Random House.
Ricoeur, P. (1994) Oneself as Another. Chicago: University of Chicago Press.

Roesler, L. (2015) A Saussurean Solution: Embodying 'Presence' in Yves Bonnefoy's Poetics. In Transnational Literature Vol 8 no 1pps 1–11.

Rohr, D. (2019) How Can Human Symbols Represent God? A Critique of and Constructive Alternative to Robert C. Neville's Account of 'Indexical' Theological Truth. In American Journal of Theology and Philosophy Vol 40 no 2 pps 73–97.

Romanyshyn R.D. (2015) Conversations in the Gap between Mind and Soul: Grammatical Reflections in (the) Place(s) of Thinking. In The Humanistic Psychologist Vol 43 no 1 pps 109–18.

Royle, N. (2000) Deconstructions: A User's Guide. Basingstoke: Palgrave.

Royle, N. (2003) Jacques Derrida. London. Routledge.

Saussure, F.de., (1916) Course in General Linguistics. New York: McGraw-Hill.

Sayegh, P.Y. (2008) Cultural Hybridity and Modern Binaries: Overcoming the Opposition between Identity and Otherness? ffhalshs-00610753f.

Schwartz-Friesel, M. (2012) On the Status of External Evidence in the Theories of Cognitive Linguistics: Compatibility Problems or Signs of Stagnation in the Field? Or: Why do Some Linguists Behave like Fodor's Input Systems? In Language Sciences Vol 34 no 6 pps 656–64.

Sheerin, D. (2009) Deleuze and Ricoeur; Disavowed Affinities and the Narrative Self. London: Continuum.

Shotter, J. (1993) M.M. Bakhtin and L.S. Vygotsky: Internalization as a Boundary Phenomenon in New Ideas. In Psychology Vol 11 no 3 pps 379–90.

Spivak, G.C. (1967) (ed. trans.) Of Grammatology. J. Derrida. Baltimore: Johns Hopkins University Press.

Spohrer, K., Stahl, G. and Bowers-Brown, T. (2018) Constituting Neoliberal Subjects? 'Aspiration' as Technology of Government in UK Policy Discourse. In Journal of Education Policy Vol 33 no 3 pps 327–42.

Tannen, D. (2009) Framing and Face; the Relevance of the Presentation of Self to Linguistic Discourse Analysis. In Social Psychology Quarterly Vol 72 no 4 pps 300–5.

Trask, R.L. (1997) The History of Basque. London and New York: Routledge.

Ullin, R.C. (2005) Social Thought and Commentary: Remembering Paul Ricoeur. In Anthropological Quarterly Vol 78 no 4 pps 885–97.

van den Hengel, J. (1994) Paul Ricoeur's 'Oneself as Another' and Practical Theology. In Theological Studies Vol 55 no 3 pps 458–80.

Vygotsky, L.S. (1978) Mind in Society; the Development of Higher Psychological Processes. Cambridge, MA: Harvard University Press.

Vygotsky, L.S. (1986) Thought and Language. Cambridge, MA: MIT Press.

Walker, C. (2019) Karl Jaspers and Karl Popper. In History of Psychiatry Vol 30 pps 172–88.

Wang, C. (2011) Power/Knowledge for Educational Theory: Stephen Ball and the Reception of Foucault. In Journal of Philosophy of Education Vol 45 no 1 pps 141–56.

Wei, L. (2016) Epilogue: Multi-competence and the Translanguaging Instinct. V. Cook and L. Wei. Cambridge UK: Cambridge University Press.
Wittgenstein, L. (1999) Tractatus Logico- Philosophicus. Mineola. New York: Dover Publications Inc.
Wittgenstein, L. (2009) Philosophical Investigations. Chichester, UK: Blackwell Publishing Ltd.
Woolf, V. (1931) The Waves. London: Penguin Random House UK.

Index

Abbinnette, R. 150
Ahmed, A. 34
Akamajian, A. 22
Almon, R. L. 114
alterity 3, 110–11, 116–22, 126, 163–5, 167–8
Amvela, E. Z. 100
Ansell-Pearson, K. 131–2
Atkin, A. 143, 146, 152
Austen, J. 164
Austin, J. L. 31, 106–8

Bache, C. 52
'Bachelor' 71
Bakhtin, M. M. 1, 88, 95–9, 114–16, 132, 141, 161–3, 165, 167
    dialogism of (*See* dialogism)
    heteroglossia (*See* heteroglossia)
    and subcultural language 99–101
basic linear grammar 39–40, 160
Basque 2, 11, 17–22, 24, 28–9, 160
Baudrillard, J. 143, 149–51, 155
Bavali, M. 15–16, 53
Bergson, H. 4, 126–34, 141–2, 145, 159
Bhabba, H. 120
blank slate 12–13, 50, 157
Bosman, N. 43–4
Bourdieu, P. 91–2
Buber, M. 103–4
Bush, S. 134, 137, 139–40

capable peers 88, 105–6
Catholics 148–9
Charlton, W. 26
Charme, S. 103
Chevalier, Y. 56–7
Chomsky, N. 1–2, 11, 14, 21–2, 25–9, 34, 37–41, 46, 50–1, 53, 79, 125. *See also* Universal Grammar (UG)
    'a priori' language module 159
    cognitive linguistics 40, 42
    ideal linguistic knowledge 13
    innate language module 50
    philosophy 27
    Poverty of Stimulus 14, 16, 27
    sentences conditions 13
Chouliaraki, L. 88, 151
Cockney Rhyming slang 70
codeswitching 169
cognitive linguistics 2, 31–2, 37–8, 40, 43–4, 46, 52, 54, 74, 160–1
    paradigms of 41–2
cognitive primitives 45
coherent identity 110, 114
commonality 6, 17, 25, 75, 90, 100–1, 135, 142
Cook, V. 168–9
Course of General Linguistics, The (Saussure) 62, 67
Covid-19 pandemic 162–3
Creative Evolution (Bergson) 126, 132
critical discourse analysis 82, 114, 151, 155–6
critical language analysis 154–5
Critique of Pure Reason (Kant) 32, 112, 158
Crowley, P. 114–15, 130
cultural
    differences 12, 30, 116–17, 119, 160
    discourse 71, 92
    diversity 11, 27
    identity 11, 57, 67, 91–2, 103, 118, 137, 165
    performance 28
    power 91

deconstruction 1, 3–6, 64, 67, 121–2, 134–40
deferral 4, 135–9, 147
Derrida, J. 1, 4, 6, 38, 132–42, 149, 167
Descartes, R. 12–13, 50, 152, 157–8, 160
dialectical relationship 79, 96, 160
dialogism 102–5
    spirituality of 103–4

differences
  cultural 12, 30, 116–17, 119, 160
  deferral and (*See* deferral)
  identity of 126
  language as 65–7
  mainstream and current social media 84
  in power 84
  sameness and 1, 6–7, 29–30, 36, 66–7, 70, 90, 156, 165, 168–70
discourse 81–2, 88–90, 92–3, 127
  critical 82, 114, 151, 155–6
  cultural 71, 92
  economic 86
  football 75
  and power 89
  power behind 82–4
  power within 85–7
  sameness in 75
  socioeconomic 85–6, 89, 92
Dornyei, Z. 119

economic discourse 86
economic power 85, 91
Edwards, R. 82–3, 147
egocentric speech 96–7, 105
English
  and Basque 2, 17–18, 20, 24, 28–30
  and French 13–14, 17, 20, 72, 135, 144, 161
  and Igala 11, 24
  monolingualism 132
  Queen's 91–2
  semantic changes 72
'escapade' 135
Essay Concerning Human Understanding (Locke) 157
ethical action 115–16
Eucharist 148–9
Evans, D. 85, 117, 166–7

Fairclough, N. 81–2, 84, 86, 88, 93, 151, 155
feminine 'elles' 56
football discourse 75
foreign language 63, 85, 103, 116–19, 161, 164, 167
formal linguistics 40–1, 49, 51, 60, 76, 80, 157, 159

Foucault, M. 38, 63–4, 81–2, 89, 92–3, 99, 106–8, 111, 114, 155, 163
freedom 15, 133–4, 141, 162–3, 169
Freire, P. 166

gender
  hierarchy 56
  social categories of 51, 56
Giardiello, P. 86
Gospel of John 70
grammar
  construe 52–3
  and lexis 51–2, 81
  linear 39–40, 54, 160
  parameters 169
  rational 2, 15, 46, 49, 90, 125
  recursive 39–40, 42, 46, 54
  social 15, 50
  surface 11, 16, 25–8, 30, 40, 51, 169
  theory of 53–5
Guilherme, A. 166
Gumperz, J. 82–3

Hahn, M. 170
Halliday, M. L. K. 14, 22, 49–53, 60, 76
  systemic functional language 15–17
Hart, C. 41, 57–8, 85
Hebert, C. 166
Heidegger, M. 17
heteroglossia 3, 88–9, 98–101, 103, 105, 107–8, 111, 120–1, 161
Holmes, J. 91
Holvoet, A. 74

ICON 144
idem/ipse dichotomy 109–11, 113, 122, 126, 164, 168
identities 89–90
  construction of 3–4
  cultural 11, 57, 67, 91–2, 103, 118, 137, 165
  hierarchy of 152–4
  and languages 1, 5–6, 17–21, 36, 46, 49, 51, 63, 97–9, 101, 107, 121, 125, 132, 135, 159, 161, 165–6, 168, 170
  layers of 24–5
  lexicogrammar and 55–7
  linguistic cultural capital 90–1
  within mind 159–61

national 112, 120
phenomenological 130-4
post-structural semiotic 149-51
rational 11, 23, 25, 31, 33-4, 52, 159
and subjectivities 163-5
subjunctive mood and 59
voices and 165
ideology 15, 24, 41, 53, 56-7, 59, 61, 67-8, 73, 81, 85, 88, 98-100, 155
Igala 2, 11, 24
sentence syntax of 21-3
imagery 43-4
indexical process 87-8
indexical sign 144, 148-9, 151-2
inner speech 96-7
interactional sociolinguistics 83, 86-8
interlocutors 82-3, 87, 101-3, 162
intersubjectivity 96-108, 113-16, 118, 130, 133, 138-9, 161-3
'I', 'Thou' relationship (Buber) 103-4

Jackendoff, R. 38, 41
linear grammar 21, 39-40, 54, 160
Parallel Architecture 40
recursive grammar 39-40, 42, 46, 54
Jackson, H. 100
Jansen, H. 113

Kant, E. 32-3, 112, 131, 146, 158-9
'Noumenon' 33, 112, 158
Kemmener, D. 22
Kumar, R. 28

Lakoff, G. 41, 44-6
Langacker, R. W. 41, 43
language
of analytical identity 154-5
cognitive linguistics 38-42
and communication 153-4
conceptual features 24-5, 43
construing 52-3
difference 65-7
English (*See* English)
French 13-14, 17, 20, 56, 72, 135, 144, 161
'House of Being' 17
identity and (*See* identity, language)

imagery and metaphor 42-5
inner and outer 28
as knowledge 13
logic of 36-8
mediaeval 63-5
rational identity of 33-4
semantic changes 71-3
Wittgenstein and 31-8, 46
Lee, B. 24
Lenneberg, E. 14
Levinas, E. 167
lexicogrammar 55-7
linear grammar 21, 39-40, 54, 160
linguistics
capacity 39, 145
cognitive (*See* cognitive linguistics)
cultural identity 90-2
diversification 98
formal 40-1, 49, 51, 60, 76, 80, 157, 159
metaprocess 28
and non-linguistic 31-2, 37-43, 45-6, 74, 159
Locke, J. 12-13, 50, 157-8

Macha, J. 34
mainstream media 84, 162
Maritain, J. 148-9
Marshall, J. D. 107
meaning slippage (slippage of meaning) 68, 69, 72, 75, 135
mediaeval language 63-5
metaidentity 17-18, 23, 170
metalinguistic identity 24, 28
metaphor 43-5, 49, 59, 61, 127, 160-1
metonymy 43
Mills, S. 88-9
misrecognition 91
mixed gender company 56-7
Modern Foreign Languages (MFL) 85, 164, 167
monolinguals 64-5, 169
multilingualism 28, 132, 165

narrative identity 3, 95, 109-11, 115-22, 125-7, 130-1, 139-40, 164-5
national identity 112, 120
natural signs 63-4, 111-12, 147-8, 152
nominalization 57-8

Ochs, E. 86–7
Order of Things, The (Foucault) 63
'Other' 95, 111, 116–20, 122, 126, 161–4, 167–8, 170

Peirce, C. S. 5, 127, 131, 143, 151
  dynamic object 147
  firstness 127–8, 131, 141, 145, 152, 164
  hierarchy of signs and identity 151–4
  secondness 131, 141, 152, 165
  signs, types of 144–7
  sign-vehicles 146
  thirdness 131, 152, 165
'People' 133
performative language 106–8, 115, 136–7
Perlina, N. 103
phenomenology 4, 126–7, 130–4
Philosophical Investigations (Wittgenstein) 34–7
Planté, C. 56–7
polysemia 134–6
Popper, K. 25, 30, 145, 152–5, 158
Port Royal grammarians 2, 13, 63
post-structuralism 113, 118, 139, 147–51, 157, 167
power 136–7, 163
prestige language 91
protolanguage 39–40
Proust, M. 55, 164

Queen's English 91–2

rational grammar 2, 15, 46, 49, 90, 125
rational identity 11, 23, 25, 33–4, 52, 159
recursive grammar 39–40, 42, 46, 54
Ricoeur, P. 3, 109–11, 121–2, 126–7, 130, 139, 164, 168
  alterity 120–1
  ethical action 115–16
  otherness 116–19
  signs 111–15
Roesler, L. 73–4
Romanyshyn, R. D. 59
Royle, N. 5–6, 136, 139–41

sameness
  and differences 1, 6–7, 29–30, 36, 66–7, 70, 90, 156, 165, 168–70
  in discourse 75
  mediaeval language of 63–5

Sapir and Wharf (Hussein) 17
Saussure, F. de. 64–5, 133, 143
  disconnection 64–5, 82
  language difference 65–7
  Langue 28, 60, 68–76, 80, 140
  linguistic sign 62, 67, 74
  Parole 28, 60, 68–75, 80, 140
  structuralism 62–3
  time 67–8
  word-sign 62–3
Sayegh, P. Y. 111
Schwartz-Friesel, M. 41–2
semantic changes
  across languages 71–3
  cultures and discourses 71
sentence conditions 13
Sheerin, D. 120–1
Shotter, J. 98
Sidighi, F. 15–16, 53
signified 36, 61, 63–5, 68, 73, 75, 79–80, 113, 131, 133, 135–6, 138–40, 143–6, 148–9
signifier 3, 36, 61, 63–5, 67–8, 73, 75, 79–80, 113, 131, 134–6, 138, 140, 143–5, 148
signs 62–4, 81, 106, 111–15, 133–4, 139–41, 146–51, 156
  hierarchy of 152–4
  natural 63–4, 111–12, 147–8, 152
  and object 143–4
  types of 144–7
'Slab' 35
social constructivism 104–6
social media 64, 84, 86, 102, 116, 125, 162–3
social power 5, 35, 80–2, 91, 125, 154
sociocultural 15, 61, 69, 76, 79–80, 82–3, 86–91, 112, 131, 153–4, 161
socioeconomic discourse 85–6, 89, 92
sociolinguistics 12, 28, 50–2, 67, 74, 76, 79–81, 87–8
'Spinster' 71
Spivak, G. C. 138
Spohrer, K. 92
Stages of Development (Piaget) 88, 95–6, 105
standard meaning 71
structuralism 62–3, 79
  post-structuralism and 147–9

structural rationality 13–14
subcultural language 99–101
subjectivity 56, 89, 95, 98, 104, 114, 126–8, 130–1, 141, 158
subject pronouns 51, 53–8, 66, 80, 87, 104, 169
subject verb object (S.V.O.) 2, 18, 21–2, 25–6
subjunctive mood 59
surface grammar 11, 16, 25–8, 30, 40, 51, 169
symbols 144, 145
syntactically grounded (Lee) 24
'systemic' 53–4, 60
systemic functional grammar 51–2
systemic functional linguistics (SFL) 52–4, 56, 59–60, 79, 159

Tannen, D. 86
third place (Bhabba) 120
Thought and Language (Vygotsky) 38–9, 96
time 62–4, 66–70, 82, 90, 103, 113, 120–2, 126, 134–7
Tractatus Logico- Philosophicus (Wittgenstein) 31–7, 61, 112, 158
translanguaging 28, 165, 168–9
Trask, R. L. 19–20
Twitter 64, 84, 101–2

Ullin, R. C. 112
unitary language 98, 100
Universal Grammar (UG) 11, 14–17, 26, 30, 40, 159–60, 169
  multilingual 168–70
  principles and parameters 26–9
  structure and content 25–6

Usher, R. 82, 147
Ushioda, E. 119

Van den Hengel, J. 109–10
verbs 58
  of motion 44–5
  tenses 12, 21, 54, 58
  transitive 18–19
Verlan 70, 100
Vygotsky, L. S. 24, 49–50, 52, 79, 88, 95–6, 98–9, 102, 107, 156, 160
  egocentric speech 96–7, 105
  inner speech 96–7
  social constructivism 104–6
  thought and language 24–5, 38, 42, 96–7

Walker, C. 25
Wang, C. 89
warning sign 144
Waves, The (Woolf) 127–9
Wei, L. 26
Wittgenstein, L. 43, 46, 61, 106–8, 131, 159
  grammar 37
  language and 31–8, 46
  language games 35–8, 46
Woolf, V. 127–30
word meanings 1, 21, 34–6, 46, 61, 67, 71–2, 76, 104, 133, 152, 154, 160–1

Yunus, R. 28

zero-sum stand-off 12
Zone of Proximal Development (Vygotsky) 88–9, 105–7

www.ingramcontent.com/pod-product-compliance
Lightning Source LLC
Chambersburg PA
CBHW061835300426
44115CB00013B/2393